AF480693

Jesus Loves Singles Too

Solo, Loved, Known By Christ

Angie C. Austin

Halen Press

ISBN: 979-8-9956442-1-7 (Hardback)

Published by Halen Press, Troy, Alabama, USA

First Edition 2026
Printed in the United States of America

Cover design by Angie C. Austin

Contact: halenpress26@gmail.com

*To my Heavenly Father and to Jesus, my Savior:
You are the source of this message, the inspiration behind every page, and the steady voice that urged me
forward.*

*To my boys: May you always experience the deep joy
and peace of being fully loved by Him.*

*To my friends and family: Thank you for drawing me
out of my shell, for helping me find my voice, and for
always including me.*

*And to every single person who feels overlooked or
doubts who they are: May you know you are cherished,
seen, and always loved.*

"For the mountains may move and the hills disappear, but even then my faithful love for you will remain. My covenant of blessing will never be broken," says the LORD who has mercy on you.
Isaiah 54:10 (NLT)

Contents

Before We Begin

Introduction

You make known to me the path of life; you will fill me with joy in your presence, with eternal pleasures at your right hand.
Psalm 16:11

The Heart Behind This Book

One day while driving, I found myself humming the simple, sweet words of a childhood song: "Jesus loves the little children"—you know the one—"all the little children of the world." As I sang it in my mind, I felt the Holy Spirit remind me of something big: His love is for everyone.

What if we replaced "little children" with other people groups?

Jesus loves the single people.

Jesus loves the married people.

Jesus loves women. Jesus loves men.

Teenagers. Families. Widows.

The overlooked. The lonely.

He loves all of us. No one is excluded.

That moment sparked the heartbeat of this book: You are who God says you are. Your identity is not shaped by your relationship status, your past, or your feelings, but by the way God sees you—with abundant joy.

You are loved, chosen, and you belong in the eyes of the One who knows you best.

Held By His Love

In today's culture, couples and marriage are often portrayed as the ultimate markers of success and fulfillment. The message is everywhere. We see it woven into TV shows, movies, social media posts, commercials, and novels. Even the tax system offers a benefit for those who check "married, filing jointly."

Messages like these leave little room to honor the beauty and purpose of singleness. They can make it seem like being single is a lesser path, like life is somehow on hold until you find "the one." But that is not true. This season can be rich with purpose, beauty, and God's handiwork in and through you—right where you are, exactly as you are.

When relationships are elevated as the gold standard of belonging, being single can feel isolating. You may feel out of place or awkward as the "odd one" at a dinner party. You might feel invisible as the person eating alone at a restaurant. I have felt that way before.

One time, I was adventurous and traveled on a cruise by myself. Listening to a string quartet before dinner, I struck up a friendly conversation with a fellow cruiser. We were talking about things we were enjoying about the trip when she eventually asked, "Didn't you have anyone in your family that would come with you?" Smiling, I explained that I did, but they were all busy. In my mind, I was thinking that I would not allow my singleness to stop me from traveling and doing things I love. God never asked me to put my joy on hold. He wants me to embrace the life He's given me.

He wants the same for you.

I wasn't always single. I was married for 13 years and became the mother of two beautiful sons. When that season ended, I stepped into a reality I never expected. Having married young, I had never really been alone. I always thought singleness meant you were waiting for life to start.

Newly solo, I searched for love, longing for companionship to fill the ache inside me. I met some good people, including one relationship that lasted seven years. But no matter how meaningful the connection, something was still missing. There was an emptiness I couldn't ignore.

It took time, heartache, and deep healing, but eventually, I discovered a peace inside. This peace did not come from a person nor a perfect relationship. It came from the One who made me, knows me, and never leaves me—Jesus.

I wish I had recognized this earlier in life: There was never anything missing. Jesus was always present with me. But to get to where I am now, I had to walk through every disappointment, every tear, and every heartbreak.

Christ is calling us to grow in Him—to live with purpose and move forward in the work He has set before us. God doesn't want us to endure singleness and just "get through it." He wants us to *thrive* in it. He wants us to live with joy, wholeness, and unwavering faith in every season of life.

Alone, Not Lonely

On social media, reality shows, and in real life, I see many amazing women and men trying so hard to belong to someone. You can sense they are searching for their worth in a soulmate. I see my old self in them.

Behind the filters, captions, and curated posts, I know what's going on beneath the surface because I have been there. Our hearts are quietly crying out: *Pick me. Choose me. Love me.* We are trying to show we have it all together by posting those smiling selfies, cheery captions, and dressed-up photos. But deep inside, we are crumbling and barely holding it together.

Each year, my pastor gives a relationship-focused series of sermons around Valentine's Day. What I appreciate is that he doesn't just talk about marriage. He thoughtfully makes space for all types of relationships—singles, dating couples, friendships, and family. I am very thankful that he recognizes everyone and every "status."

There was a year when I felt especially lonely during one of these services. At just the right moment, my pastor looked out at the congregation to address the single people. He said something that I will never forget: "Why are you trying so hard to find love from someone else? You are the daughter of a King who adores you!"

That hit me deep.

I thought, "You are right, Pastor! Why am I so sad to be alone? I am God's pride and joy!" This is the most genuine and truest love.

In a therapy session, my counselor gave some advice that changed my direction. She said, "You need to learn to live alone, not lonely." I was on the verge of becoming a solo empty nester and her words gave me a fresh perspective on my life. As a result, I began my journey of living "alone" without the "lonely" part. Along the way, I came to love God more deeply with greater intention.

I have been a Christian since I was a young child, so I have always known that God loves me. But in this season of singleness, His love became real in a brand new way. It wasn't just something I heard preached in sermons. It was something I experienced firsthand.

I have come to understand that my wholeness is found in Him. He is the One who truly fills my heart. The emptiness I once believed was there does not exist, because with Jesus, I have ALWAYS been complete. I am rooted in His perfect, unconditional love—and nothing could be better.

Filled With Joy

We may not know what the future holds, but we can be confident in the One who holds it: Jesus. He is where our hearts and lasting joy are found. Our lives might include a partner in good time, or we could experience more seasons of being solo. No matter what lies ahead, we can always trust the One who writes our stories.

Scripture reminds us that our identity and worth are rooted in something far more profound than our relationship status or life circumstances. We are anchored in our relationship with God.

Colossians 3:3 assures that our "life is now hidden with Christ in God." This verse reveals that our value is secure in our union with Jesus. He is our source of life, purpose, and lasting hope. When we embrace this, we discover a peace that consumes our souls.

You can walk on the life path God has set before you with your head held high. He will instill a calmness in your heart and confidence in your mind. When you embrace His love, trust His timing, and rest in Him, those empty, hollow feelings will be replaced with the joy of being completely known and loved.

An Invitation

In a world that measures worth by relationship status or social milestones, this book is a gentle invitation to see yourself through a different lens—the loving eyes of God. The heart behind these pages is to remind you that your value is not determined by who you are with, but by who you are in Christ. Scripture affirms this truth over and over. You are deeply rooted (Ephesians 3:17), eternally chosen (Ephesians 1:4), and wonderfully made (Psalm 139:14).

Singleness does not have to be a sentence of sadness. Instead, it can be a sacred space where God's love meets you most intimately. His affection isn't second-best or a temporary filler. It is the truest, most lasting love you will ever know. He wants you to know that you are not forgotten, nor overlooked. You are the daughter or son of a King—loved, known, and never alone.

My sincere hope is that you will be uplifted and transformed by God's unwavering love as you read this book. May He bless your heart, mind, and soul. You didn't pick up this book by accident—you were led here by the Creator Himself!

Each chapter concludes with affirmations to anchor your heart in truth. They also contain reflection questions to help you expand your thinking by writing about your journey. These are designed to remind you of who you are and whose you are—*every single day*.

My Prayer for You

Dear Heavenly Father,

Thank You for Your beautiful, everlasting love. I lift up the person reading these words. You know exactly why they have arrived here at this specific moment in time. I pray that they open their heart, soul, and mind to You. Whatever season they are in, I ask You to meet them with Your peace and guidance. Remind them that they are never alone because You are always near. Help them to know, that they are precious in Your sight.

Amen.

Who You Are: Established in Love and Grace

Part One

*We know how much God loves us, and we have put
our trust in his love. God is love, and all who
live in love live in God, and God lives in them.
1 John 4:16 (NLT)*

Chapter One

You Are Rooted in Love

*And I pray that you, being rooted and established in love,
may have power, together with all the Lord's holy people, to
grasp how wide and long and high and deep is the love of
Christ, and to know this love that surpasses knowledge—that
you may be filled to the measure of all the fullness of God.*
Ephesians 3:16–19

Strong and Steady

I live along the Gulf Coast, where hurricanes are no
strangers. We have had our fair share over the years. They
always begin the same with rising anticipation and a sense of
unrest.

Of the storms I have weathered, Hurricane Sally was one of the
worst. She moved painfully slow, less than five miles per hour.
She crept in during the night and camped over our house for
nearly twelve hours. Like an unwanted guest who overstayed
their welcome, she lingered and would not leave!

The rain felt endless. And the wind, oh, the wind! It howled
without pause. We could hear and feel thuds of tree limbs
crashing against the house and roof.

My neighborhood is filled with oak trees, fitting, because it is named Mighty Oaks. One of the biggest stands in the backyard. It is massive and towers over my house. The branches stretch wide, leaving a canopy that feels protective.

I was especially worried about that tree during the storm. It isn't just tall—it is beautiful. And it is extremely strong. A fixture of peace and strength in my everyday life.

When the sun finally came up and Miss Sally had departed, I walked outside to assess the damage. Thankfully, it was minimal. The small tree in the front yard had split in half. A few shingles were missing from the roof. The privacy fence had tumbled over. And the backyard was covered in leaves and limbs.

But the mighty oak?

She was still standing, strong and beautiful as ever. That was no surprise. Oak trees slowly develop deep, adaptable roots that spread far beyond what the eye can see, sometimes three times wider than the canopy.

Their strength isn't sudden or flashy. It is built quietly over years. Long before branches stretch skyward, roots are forming below the surface. That unseen foundation is what keeps the tree firmly planted when storms rage.

Your spiritual strength is similar. It takes precious time to grow. Just as roots deepen gradually beneath the surface, your faith is formed in quiet, faithful moments. Through prayer, unhurried time in God's presence, and reading His Word, your spiritual roots begin to stretch downward. Much of this growth happens un-seen—on ordinary days when nothing dramatic seems to change.

Yet with time, those hidden moments matter. As your roots deepen, you develop a steady connection to Christ, one that doesn't depend on circumstances or emotions. You become grounded in a love that isn't shallow or shifting, but firm, faithful, and secure. And when storms come—as they always do—you discover that your strength was being built long before you realized you would need it.

The Experience of Perfect Love

We know God loves us, but how do we know? And more than that, how do we experience His love?

For me, it is hard to explain with words alone. God's love isn't just something I understand in my head. It is something I feel deep in my heart. It's a peace that settles over my mind, soul, and spirit. A calm assurance that I am never alone. That assurance comes from the Holy Spirit.

When we become Christians, God gives us the gift of the Holy Spirit who dwells within us (John 14:26). This Advocate doesn't come and go—He stays. Romans 5:5 brings it to light:

> *And hope does not put us to shame, because God's love has been poured out into our hearts through the Holy Spirit, who has been given to us.*

The Holy Spirit, our helper, supports us in many ways. In addition to being our Advocate, He is our counselor, strengthener, and intercessor (John 14:16; Romans 8:26). He convicts us when we begin to wander away from Jesus (John 16:8). He reminds us that our identity is rooted in God's love (Romans 5:5). He teaches us quietly as we read and reflect on Scripture (John 14:26; 1 Corinthians 2:10–13). And He comforts us when we feel forgotten or alone (John 14:18; 2 Corinthians 1:3–4). This constant presence is where peace and joy come from.

When I am feeling down or all alone, the Holy Spirit reminds me that I'm not. He tells me that I am a beloved child of God—that I am special in His sight.

In what ways does He do this?

Sometimes a verse will come into my mind and cover my heart—the exact words I didn't know I needed. Other times, it is a friend or family member who calls unexpectedly, just to check in. They have no idea they are answering a prayer I never said out loud.

There are also moments when a meaningful song comes on the radio at just the right second. It feels as though heaven timed it perfectly. And then there are the small, quiet signs: a red bird flying past my window or a breathtaking sunset that feels too intentional to ignore.

He shows up in so many beautiful, unexpected ways. Not always loud or dramatic, but always personal.

Another way to experience God's love is through reading the Bible. When you spend time resting in His Word, you will see how much He cares about you. Through reading stories, psalms, and promises, you will feel His adoration. It feeds love into your heart.

My relationship with God grew stronger when I committed to reading the entire Bible from cover to cover. I use a yearly plan, which directs me to read a few chapters each day. With each one, my eyes open to new truths and insights. His Word keeps me connected, guides my steps, and gives me peace. I love to read it because it gives me opportunities to discover more.

The Bible is a love story between God and His people. Throughout Scripture, He blesses, protects, and remains sovereign over every detail of their lives. And the best part? That love wasn't just for Israel. It also reaches out to all of us including you and me—His love is for everyone. What a gift!

Firmly Planted

In the early part of singlehood, I found myself searching for someone to root my love in—someone I could pour my energy into. But time after time, it ended in disappointment, confusion, and heartbreak. I spent a tremendous amount of time wondering why my potential partner didn't want me back. It became a familiar story with changing faces: same song, different verse. I was chasing approval and affection from people who were never meant to fill that space in my heart.

When we seek love from people who do not or cannot respond, we are left feeling empty and heartbroken. But God's love is unique and entirely different.

In Him, we are seen, known, and loved—completely.

His love offers the security and confidence our hearts crave. We never have to worry about being ghosted or abandoned. God is present and always reaching for us.

He makes it clear that He loves us—fully, perfectly, and unconditionally. With Him, we are never unsure of where we stand. His love never disappoints. Moses' statement in Deuteronomy 31:8 serves as a reminder:

> ***"The LORD himself goes before you and will be with you; he will never leave you nor forsake you. Do not be afraid; do not be discouraged."***

That is something we can rely on.

The apostle Paul put it this way in his letter to the believers in Rome:

> ***For I am convinced that neither death nor life, neither angels nor demons, neither the present nor the future, nor any powers, neither height nor depth, nor anything else in all creation, will be able to separate us from the love of God that is in Christ Jesus our Lord*** (Romans 8:38–39).

Paul listed extreme contrasts to paint a detailed picture of God's vast love for His children. He wanted the people to grasp just how deep, wide, and unwavering that love truly is.

When we are grounded in His love, every piece of our heart is full. This makes all the difference—from how we live to how we view ourselves. Instead of striving for the approval of people who may never see our worth, we begin to seek His will and His view of us. That shift sets us free.

Nothing can separate you from the love of your King. *Nothing.*

Even when we sin, His love remains—unshaken and unconditional. Like a loving parent, He will discipline and guide us back on the right course. He even redeems our failures, weaving them into His greater good.

When life feels shaky, God's love is not. It is certain. You can trust Him. His presence will steady and calm your soul when everything around you seems to be changing.

To be this securely loved—whether single, dating, or married—is the unshakable foundation our hearts long for. That is the gift of being rooted in Him.

My Prayer For You

Dear Heavenly Father,

Thank You for the person reading this prayer. I ask that they would experience the fullness of Your love in a personal way. May they be grounded in it like a mighty tree that stands firm through a storm. Remind them that Your love does not fade with time or circumstances. It is constant, faithful, and everlasting. Let them find their security and worth in You.

Amen.

Daily Affirmations

    1. I am grounded in God's unwavering love.

    2. God's love is not based on my relationship status.

    3. I am fully known by my Heavenly Father.

Reflections

    1. Are there quiet places in your life where you can pause and experience God's presence?

    2. How does knowing you are rooted in God's love affect the way you view your worth?

Chapter Two

You Are Chosen

*For you are a people holy to the LORD your God. The
LORD your God has chosen you out of all the peoples on
the face of the earth to be his people, his treasured possession.*
Deuteronomy 7:6

The Last One

I was not the most athletic person in school. Not. Even. Close.

In my primary years, I was usually one of the last students picked for a team at PE. It happened more times than I care to count. Those hot, steamy days on the playground were not fun for me.

Middle school PE wasn't much better. One time, the coach grouped all of the band students together on one team, which included me. We affectionately named ourselves the "Bandos." We made two baskets for the entire season scoring a grand total of four points. And you know what? We were proud of that!

And then there was high school. I played tennis but lacked a fierce, competitive edge. I did not have the "warrior" mindset you see in top athletes. On the occasion that I did hit the ball out of my opponent's reach, I would yell, "I'm sorry!"

The sting of being picked last didn't end there. It followed me into adulthood when navigating all of those dating apps. Talk about being overwhelmed! Too many questions to answer and an overload of pictures to swipe on. When someone that I was interested in would not respond, conflicting feelings stirred in my mind.

Will he ever swipe for me?

Why won't he write back?

Is he choosing someone else?

What can I do to make him like me?

Thoughts like these creep in quietly, but turn into loud screams. If we are not careful, the questions shape how we view ourselves. They can leave us feeling unworthy, insignificant, and not good enough. Before we realize it, we have developed a negative self image.

Can you relate to thoughts like these? Thoughts that leave you with a sinking feeling that maybe—just maybe— you are not what people are looking for?

Our Heavenly Father would never make us feel that way. He does not plant seeds of insecurity in our heads. His voice speaks love, not doubt. With God, we are chosen—***always***.

He will not leave us standing last on the playground or ignored on the gym court. He won't scroll by our profile on an app. He is not seeking perfection, nor is He concerned with how flawless we appear in our social media posts.

Our God extends His hand—steady, faithful, full of grace—and invites us into a relationship. He looks beyond our surface and searches the depths of our souls. He sees our hearts, and lovingly chooses us exactly as we are.

Handpicked

Have you ever struggled to find a gift for someone you love? You want to find the perfect thing: the best color, the best design, the best price. So many decisions to make! When you finally decide, you realize that you have spent a great deal of time and energy being overly picky and selective.

With God, it is different. He chooses every one of us. He sees all of us as the "just right" and "perfect" gift—no wasting time in making a decision. He doesn't think twice about it.

Out of love, He calls each one of us into a relationship with Him. No one is left out or waiting to be selected for the team. No one is waiting to be chosen on a dating app. We are all invited and eagerly accepted. His outstretched hand is always reaching and saying, *I choose you*.

God's decision to choose you and me has nothing to do with our performance, our achievements, or whether we deserve it. It is entirely due to His loving kindness. Being chosen by Him is divine and sacred. It is a testament to your worth and His love for you.

> **But you are a chosen people, a royal priesthood, a holy nation, God's special possession, that you may declare the praises of him who called you out of darkness into his wonderful light.** (1 Peter 2:9)

Through Jesus, the invitation is permanent, never to be taken away. His sacrifice made it possible for us to be part of God's family. When we say "yes" to Him, we are set apart to reflect His glory. We are His very own children and precious in His sight.

We can live knowing that our identity is secure in Him and Him alone. It is not based on other people's opinions or our relationship status. His love is a constant, immovable stone (1 Peter 2:6) upon which we can always rely, regardless of our circumstances or feelings.

I have been left heartbroken by people I once chose—people I tried to build my heart around. I rooted my identity, security, and worth in them. But time and time again, I was left disappointed and unfulfilled. Instead of joy, there were many tears and lots of confusion. Have you ever been there?

If someone makes you feel unchosen, unseen, or unworthy, they are not God's pick for you. You may feel the urge to rush into a relationship, but God's peace reminds us: His timing is different, His plans are good, and He knows what He is doing. We can trust *that in all things God works for the good of those who love him, who have been called according to his purpose* (Romans 8:28).

A Chosen King

There's someone in the Bible we can relate to: David, son of Jesse. You might remember him as being the one who defeated and brought down the mighty Goliath (1 Samuel 17). Before the giant-slaying and the songs of victory, David was simply the youngest son in his family. He was the one everyone was most likely to overlook.

While his seven older brothers were admired as strong, valiant warriors, David's life looked different. He was a shepherd and a musician, quietly tending his father's sheep in the hills of Bethlehem. Day after day, he protected them with courage and tenderness while his heart was turned toward the God he loved so deeply.

The day came when King Saul's heart had grown to be full of stubborn pride. He refused to listen to the Lord, follow His commands, or turn from sin. That's when God charted a different course.

He sent the prophet Samuel to Bethlehem to anoint a new king from Jesse's family of the tribe of Judah. The older sons lined up, and one by one, Jesse proudly presented them. Samuel was impressed. Each one looked the part, but they weren't the right fit. With every contender, God's voice was clear: *Not this one.*

Meanwhile, David was in the pasture doing his job, forgotten by everyone—except God. Samuel asked if there were any other sons, and only then did Jesse mention David. When David arrived, God confirmed, *"This is the one"* (1 Samuel 16:12b).

***So Samuel took the horn of oil and anointed him in the presence of his brothers, and from that day on the Spirit of the LORD came powerfully upon David.* (1 Samuel 16:13)**

As we can see, one of the most significant kings in history—an ancestor of Jesus Himself (Matthew 1)—once felt completely unchosen. David was the youngest and overlooked by his father. He did not even get an invitation to stand with his brothers. But God looked past David's appearance and saw his humble heart, quiet faith, and deep devotion (1 Samuel 16:7). Ultimately, God handpicked him.

As a shepherd, David spent many quiet moments in the pasture. He had ample time to think and reflect in solitude. Maybe you are in a similar season, especially if you are navigating singleness or waiting for your life to unfold in a certain way. These times feel like they are moving at a snail's pace, weighed down by loneliness, confusion, and unanswered questions. I imagine David wrestled with the same emotions.

The time spent in the pasture was not wasted for David. It actually prepared him. In the same way, this season of singleness might leave you feeling invisible, but it could be where God is shaping your heart for something greater.

God saw David, inside and out. And He sees you too! He knows your heart. He sees your faith, your quiet acts of love, your tears, your hopes. If you are ever feeling invisible or discouraged, I encourage you to return to this beautiful story in 1 Samuel 16.

More Than OK

It's OK to be single and it's OK to be alone. Society may try to convince you that you are unworthy because you do not have a partner but that could not be further from the truth. God did not forget you. He picked you!

When you feel invisible, please know that you are never overlooked. You can walk with confidence and boldness, knowing in your heart that the King of Kings chooses you. He holds the road map for your life and has a purpose designed just for you. His ways are higher, and He has good plans, even when you can't yet see the outcome.

God does not want you to feel sad or less-than because you are walking this season without a significant other. He wants you to celebrate it! He wants you to be filled with joy in all that you do as you walk with Him (Psalm 16:11).

You can accomplish a great deal during this time of being single. Find your joy. Find your purpose. Ask Him to reveal it, and trust that He will in His perfect timing.

Be sensitive to the leading of the Holy Spirit and stay alert to what He is whispering to your heart. You can live with purpose and intention, because He has plans for you and they are divinely perfect.

My Prayer For You

Dear Heavenly Father,

Thank You for the invitation into a relationship with You. I lift up this friend and pray they remember You have handpicked them with love. You want them to live with joy no matter their relationship status. Surround them with signs of Your love through others and quiet moments with You. Give them peace knowing You choose them with grace.

Amen.

Daily Affirmations

1. God chooses me.

2. I am not overlooked or forgotten.

3. I am handpicked by Jesus.

Reflections

1. What truth from this chapter speaks most to your heart?

2. How can you walk confidently knowing that God chooses you?

Chapter Three

You Are Seen and Heard

She gave this name to the LORD who spoke to her: "You are the God who sees me," for she said, "I have now seen the One who sees me."
Genesis 16:13

In Plain Sight

I can't tell you how many times I have searched for something, only to find it was right in front of me all along. Take for example: my phone. I have been known to search for it everywhere, only to find it ringing from my back pocket!

My sons do this too, especially when they are scavenging the fridge or pantry for a snack. One of them is a ketchup lover. There was an evening he stared into the refrigerator and said, "Mom, I can't find the ketchup!" I walked over, and sure enough, it was right there. Front and center. "Oh, I didn't even see it!" he laughed.

These moments can make us feel silly, but also strangely seen. It is easy to miss what is right in front of us when life is busy and our minds are juggling work, kids, and endless to-do lists. If your eyes are blurry from stress or lack of sleep, it can be hard to notice the obvious.

Sometimes we feel like the ones hidden in plain sight—right there in the middle of everything, yet somehow overlooked. I am blessed with wonderful friends and family who love me, and I love them dearly in return. Yet even in a room full of people who care about me, there are moments when I feel unseen. It is a strange experience to be physically present and still feel as though no one notices you.

I recall a girls' trip with some of my closest and oldest friends. We were out enjoying dinner, sharing stories and laughter. They were swapping sweet stories about their husbands and marriages. Nothing dramatic, just life, love, and connection. I sat there with nothing to contribute. I felt left out.

To be clear, it was not my friends' fault that I felt that way. It was the enemy who slithered in quietly and unnoticed. They had included me 100%—kind and loving as always. Still, in that moment, I felt isolated, unseen, and unheard. Even in the middle of love and laughter, that familiar ache crept in.

Have you ever felt that way? Like you're standing in the middle of the room, but no one sees you?

You are not the only one. Throughout Scripture, we see people who felt invisible and alone—yet none of them truly were. Our Heavenly Father was with each one of them. Let's explore a few of those moments together.

He Sees You

In the early chapters of Genesis, we meet Hagar, an Egyptian servant in the household of Sarai, the wife of Abram (who would later be renamed Abraham). Sarai (later renamed Sarah) had been unable to conceive a child. In her desperation to build a family, she offered Hagar to Abram as a secondary wife, hoping that Hagar could bear a child on her behalf.

After Hagar became pregnant, something changed. Scripture tells us that she began to despise Sarai—maybe feeling superior, maybe resenting how she'd been used. Whatever the reason, their relationship quickly broke down. Sarai, hurt and angry, blamed Abram and began to treat Hagar harshly in return.

What did Hagar do? She ran. Pregnant and alone, she fled into the wilderness.

And that's precisely where God found her.

In the middle of nowhere, in the middle of her pain, God met her personally. He called her by name. He saw her heart and gave her a promise regarding the child she was carrying. In response, Hagar gave God a name: *El Roi*—*"the God who sees me"* (Genesis 16:13).

Hagar felt overlooked by the people in her life—but God saw her. In the wilderness of being unseen, Hagar discovered the One who always sees.

Her story reminds us that even when no one else seems to notice, we are never invisible to God. The God who saw Hagar sees you, too. He knows your name, your story, and your heart.

Take a moment to reflect: What part of your life do you most need Him to notice right now?

Invite Him into that space. Even in this single season of life, He sees you and notices you. He wants to help you. He lovingly invites you to come to His feet and lay your burdens down. Just like

Hagar, you do not have to walk through this season alone. You can confidently move forward knowing that you are seen, valued, and secure in His love.

Reaching for the One

Imagine having no friends. No family. No one who cares about you. When strangers see you coming, they turn and walk the other way. No one wants to talk to you. No one offers a quick smile, wave, or "hello there." It is hard to fathom that happening in today's world. But that is what happened to a woman we read about in the Gospels of Matthew, Mark, and Luke.

There was a woman who had suffered from a bleeding disorder for twelve years. According to Jewish law, she was considered ritually unclean. She was physically, emotionally, and spiritually isolated—painfully cut off from her community. Just imagine people running the opposite way when they saw her coming. It is heartbreaking to think about.

She had seen many doctors and spent all she had in hope of finding a cure. But nothing worked. Not only did her condition remain: It grew worse.

Then, at her lowest moment, hope appeared.

She heard that Jesus would be passing by on His way to Jerusalem. She believed she would be healed if she could be in His presence. She simply wanted to be near Him.

Talk about faith that moves mountains.

As Jesus walked through the streets of Capernaum, crowds pressed in. Think of a packed theme park, a concert, or a sold-out sporting event—that kind of crowd. People everywhere were just hoping to catch a tiny glimpse of Him.

But this woman wanted more than a simple glance. She was determined and her faith was bold. Somehow, she pushed her way through the mass and reached Him.

> *She came up behind him in the crowd and touched his cloak, because she thought, "If I just touch his clothes, I will be healed." Immediately her bleeding stopped and she felt in her body that she was freed from her suffering. (Mark 5:27-29).*

Did you catch that?

The bleeding stopped. Immediately.

Jesus turned to the crowd and asked,

> *"Who touched my clothes?"* (Mark 5:30)

Imagine the whole street suddenly going still, so quiet you could hear a pin drop. The disciples were confused. With all the people pressing in, it was an odd question. Surely someone had just bumped into Him?

Jesus knew this was different. He felt power leave His body (Mark 5:30).

The woman knew what happened. Trembling, she came forward and fell at His feet. She was afraid—afraid of being judged, rejected, or worse. Bravely, she chose not to hide. She told the truth.

Jesus did not scold her. He did not push her away or call her out for interrupting. Instead, He welcomed her:

> **"Daughter, your faith has healed you. Go in peace and be freed from your suffering" (Mark 5:34).**

This is such a wonderful testimony in the Bible. It reveals Jesus' genuine compassion and kindness. When no one else saw this defeated woman, He did. He did not judge or rebuke her. He lovingly blessed and accepted her. He made her feel included.

As a solo, you may sometimes feel like the woman with the bleeding disorder—invisible, lonely, and heartbroken.

But hear this clearly: Those thoughts are not from God. It is the enemy trying to wear you down, whispering lies that attack your worth and confidence.

To fight back, you must ground yourself in the truth. Just like the woman in the crowd, you can have faith in the One who *always sees you.*

Some days will not be easy, and that's okay. Do not be discouraged if the struggle feels long. When emotions rise and you begin to feel overlooked or forgotten, turn your heart toward God's goodness and grace. You can:

- Pray honestly and boldly.

- Reflect on Scripture, especially the Psalms. They are full of reminders that you are seen, heard, and loved.

- Listen to uplifting music that speaks truth to your soul.

- Call a trusted friend or family member who can remind you that you are not alone.

- And most importantly, remember this promise and write it on your heart: God is the One who sees you.

Quiet Faith, Hidden Hope

Joseph's life is a poignant reminder of what it means to trust God in the midst of waiting. He was cast aside by those who should have loved him the most: his brothers.

Joseph was favored by his father, Jacob, and his brothers resented him for it. Their jealousy grew stronger when Jacob gave him a richly ornamented robe (Genesis 37:3).

To rid themselves of Joseph, the brothers initially plotted to kill him. Instead, they sold him into slavery to a caravan of traveling traders headed to Egypt. The brothers returned home with Joseph's torn, bloodied robe, leading Jacob to believe a wild animal had killed his beloved son. The deception shattered Jacob's heart and Joseph's life as he knew it was gone.

In Egypt, Joseph was sold to Potiphar, a high-ranking official in Pharaoh's court. Though Joseph worked with integrity, he was falsely accused by Potiphar's wife and thrown into prison.

In a dark and forgotten cell, Joseph continued to walk in faith. He interpreted dreams for two fellow prisoners: the royal cupbearer and the baker. Joseph asked the cupbearer to remember him once he was released (Genesis 40:14), but the cupbearer forgot. Once again, Joseph was overlooked.

Joseph waited. Days turned into weeks. Weeks turned into months. And months turned into years. Still, he trusted.

After the long wait, Joseph was summoned by Pharaoh to interpret a troublesome dream. Joseph's interpretation was spot on, and in God's perfect timing, things transformed. Pharaoh was pleased and elevated Joseph to second-in-command over all of Egypt. Joseph's quiet years of faithfulness in obscurity prepared him for his new assignment.

Sometime later, a severe famine struck Canaan, and Joseph's brothers traveled to Egypt to purchase grain. They stood before a powerful Joseph, unaware that he was the brother they had once betrayed. They saw him, but did not recognize him. *He was hidden in plain sight.*

Joseph knew exactly who they were.

When the time came to reveal the truth, Joseph's response was not one of revenge, but of grace. His brothers braced for judgment. But instead of condemnation, Joseph offered forgiveness. He saw the hand of God at work through every painful chapter of his life. He told them:

> *"And now, do not be distressed and do not be angry with yourselves for selling me here, because it was to save lives that God sent me ahead of you. For two years now there has been famine in the land, and for the next five years there will be no plowing and reaping. But God sent me ahead of you to preserve for you a remnant on earth and to save your lives by a great deliverance"* **(Genesis 45:5-7).**

Joseph's story teaches us that faithfulness in the shadows is not wasted. Scripture does not detail all of his inner thoughts, but we can imagine the emotional weight he carried: betrayal, abandonment, loneliness, and loss—all feelings we might experience in a solo season. Still, he chose to respond with forgiveness, hope, and love. He could not control what happened to him, but he could choose how he responded. And he did so with unwavering trust in God.

Like Joseph, we may find ourselves in seasons of waiting, wondering when the breakthrough will come. It is easy to feel overlooked or forgotten when we are single. But we are not. God sees us and is with us through every step. He is always working for us, even when we do not realize it.

There is no need to put our lives on hold. We can live with purpose right now serving in churches, encouraging coworkers, volunteering in our communities, or simply showing kindness to someone who needs it. Every act of love and service reflects God's heart to the world.

When we live with faithfulness and intention, we are reminded that God is present in the waiting. He sees and hears us. He loves us. And He is writing a greater story—*through every season.*

My Prayer For You

Dear Heavenly Father,

Wrap this precious reader in Your love and remind them that they are fully seen and known by You. When they feel invisible or forgotten, remind their heart that You have never taken Your eyes off them. Let them sense Your presence in the ordinary. Help them to walk in confidence, knowing that You see them, hear them, and call them by name.

Amen.

Daily Affirmations

1. God sees me.

2. God hears me.

3. I am valued.

Reflections

1. Which person in this chapter do you identify with most?

2. How does knowing that God sees and hears you help you in your current season?

Chapter Four

You Are Adored

For the Lord takes delight in his people; he crowns the humble with victory.
Psalm 149:4

He Really Likes You

We hear that God loves us—over and over. We believe it in theory. If we are honest, sometimes that love can feel distant or dutiful, like He's obligated to care for us because He is God.

But what if the truth is more personal? What if God doesn't just love you—what if He *adores* you? What if He enjoys who you are, delights in your presence, and sings over you with joy?

There are moments in life when we feel deeply adored. If you have ever been the guest of honor at a surprise party, you know exactly what I mean. You stand at the door, unaware of what is on the other side. When you walk in, people start cheering your name, tossing confetti, and doing silly dances. They are there just for *you*.

Maybe your pets shower you with that kind of love when returning home from a long trip. If you have a dog, it might jump, spin in circles, and give you those wet sloppy kisses. It is more than excited to be near you and truly happy that you are home.

Every day moments like these resemble a holy affirmation: God doesn't just love you; He delights in you and wants to be near you. He desires to be a part of every aspect of your life. Zephaniah 3:17 provides a beautiful description:

> ***The LORD your God is with you, the Mighty Warrior who saves. He will take great delight in you; in his love, he will no longer rebuke you, but will rejoice over you with singing.***

How cool is that? He sings over you! Not only does He care, but He rejoices when you are near! His eyes light up when you enter His presence. He beams over you.

We see this kind of affection in Jesus' baptism. Before He performed a single miracle or preached His first sermon, God declared:

> ***"This is my Son, whom I love; with Him I am well pleased"* (Matthew 3:17).**

Living single does not mean you are living unloved. In fact, it is quite the opposite. You are in a season where you can fully experience God's affection and adoration.

Stay alert for moments where God shows His delight in your daily routine. It could be a surprise from a friend, a beautiful sunset, or a hobby that sparks joy. These are ways He says, *I adore and treasure you.*

Unconditional Love

In today's world, busyness is often linked to being valued. If we do more at work or pack all that we can into a 24-hour day, we think we'll be praised, needed, and loved more. We push ourselves toward burnout, giving everything to everyone and leaving nothing for ourselves. Social media adds to the pressure. Likes, comments, and curated highlight reels affirm us.

But God does not work that way. You do not have to do more to be more in His eyes. He loves you without conditions and delights in your unfiltered, quiet self. He sees the real you and declares, *You are already enough.*

We see this lived out in one of Jesus' close friends: Mary of Bethany.

In Luke 10:38–42, we meet two sisters, Martha and Mary. As Jesus and His disciples traveled through their village, Martha opened their house. She was in a whirlwind of cooking, cleaning, and preparing everything just right.

This kind of hustle and bustle brings back fond memories of my grandmother on Christmas Day zipping around the kitchen, making sure every detail of lunch was perfect. The table was set with care, the food was warm and delicious, and the house was welcoming. It was her way of showing love to our entire family—through service and effort. Martha probably felt the same way.

Where was Mary during this preparation? Well, she was not helping Martha. She was not assisting her at all. Instead, she was sitting at Jesus' feet, captivated by His words. She was enjoying being in His presence and listening to His teachings.

Frustrated and overly exhausted, Martha asked Jesus to tell Mary to lend a hand with the work. Jesus did not respond as she expected. Instead, He replied:

***"Mary has chosen what is better, and it will not be taken away from her"* (Luke 10:42).**

He did not dismiss Martha's service. Instead, He honored Mary's stillness.

Mary was not trying to earn Jesus' approval. Nor was she striving to prove her worth. She just wanted to be near Him—and that was enough. In a world that rewarded hustle, she chose presence. And Jesus praised her for it.

So what can we learn from this moment?

Mary's choice teaches us that our worth is rooted deeply and securely in God's love. When we are single, it can be easy to feel the pressure to prove ourselves—to show the world that we are desirable, valuable, and successful. We strain to be noticed, hoping that if we do enough, achieve enough, or become enough, someone will finally see us.

But we do not have to live that way.

Because the truth is this: You are already seen, known, and fully accepted by Jesus. His eyes were on you long before anyone else's opinion ever mattered. He loves you exactly as you are—not for what you produce, not for how impressive you are, and not for whether you are chosen by another person.

You don't have to strive or hustle for visibility, nor do you have to exhaust yourself trying to prove your worth. You can rest—because the God who created you, the Savior who redeemed you, has already called you precious, valuable, and deeply loved.

Take a cue from Mary: Slow down, be present, and allow yourself to be seen by God. Knowing in your heart that He takes great delight in you will bring forth peace, freedom, and a deep sense of worth.

The Enemy's Lie

If you have ever been lied to by someone you trusted, you know how painful it feels. Lies wound deeply and target the heart. They leave scars that cannot be erased and questions that linger.

The enemy works the same way. He is the master deceiver—the father of lies (John 8:44). His goal is to twist the truth just enough to make us doubt God. He sneaks in quietly and unnoticed, poking at our weak spots. He whispers things like: *If God really adored you, you wouldn't be alone. You're missing out. You are not enough without someone else.*

Lies sting. They can be especially painful and very personal when we are navigating a solo life. They press on tender places in our hearts. Unlike people who may have been dishonest with you, **God never lies.** His words are steady, faithful, and true.

When lies cause you to question your worth, let God rewrite the story. He says: *"You are precious and honored in my sight"* (Isaiah 43:4) and *"I have loved you with an everlasting love"* (Jeremiah 31:3).

The enemy's lie leaves you feeling empty and rejected. God's truth fills you with peace and belonging. One imprisons; the other frees.

When you hear the enemy's voice telling you that you are forgotten, remember this: God genuinely *adores* you. Every word He speaks over you is life and love.

Picture This

Imagine walking into a crowded room. You have a heavy heart. A special someone ended up letting you down in a big way. As a result, you have overwhelming feelings of sadness and despair. You feel a great loss of hope.

You glance around the room and find a familiar face.

It is Jesus.

He lights up when he sees you. There is no disappointment in His eyes. Just joy. He is sincerely happy that you arrived. He sees the pain behind your smile. He knows the loneliness, the rejection, and He feels it with you. His compassion flows like a healing stream.

As you stand with Him, everything changes: The weight lifts, warmth blooms and joy bubbles up from deep inside. You are seen and deeply adored.

Let this thought settle within your heart. Don't just imagine it—*believe it*. It is one hundred percent true! Speak these words over yourself as a reminder of who you are and how deeply you are cherished:

- I am deeply loved and delighted in by Jesus. He takes great joy in me.

- He sees me, knows me, and smiles when I walk into the room.

- I am not alone in my pain. He is near to the brokenhearted (Psalm 34:18).

- I do not have to earn His affection. His love is steadfast and unchanging (Jeremiah 31:3).

When you begin to believe these declarations from God, your heart redirects. You stop looking for adoration elsewhere because you realize that you already have it. It has been with you all along.

In a season when you may not be celebrated by a significant other, don't forget: God sees you with delight. You are the apple of His eye (Psalm 17:8) and His treasured one. You are always loved and always adored. Let the Holy Spirit lay these declarations on your heart. They will bring forth great peace and joy.

My Prayer for You

Dear Jesus,

Thank You for adoring this friend. Help them know that You love them exactly as they are. May they feel valued and deeply treasured by You. Please silence the inner critic that says they must perform to prove their worth. Remind them that they are already enough because they belong to You.

Amen.

Daily Affirmations

1. God adores me.

2. Jesus delights in me.

3. I am the apple of His eye.

Reflections

1. How can knowing God adores you change the way you view your single season?

2. Picture Jesus' face lighting up when He sees you. Write down what you imagine He would say to you in that moment.

Why You Matter: Purpose in Your Present Season

Part Two

"For I know the plans I have for you," says the LORD. "They are plans for good and not for disaster, to give you a future and a hope."
Jeremiah 29:11 (NLT)

Chapter Five

You Are Important

For we are God's masterpiece. He has created us anew in Christ Jesus, so we can do the good things he planned for us long ago.
Ephesians 2:10 (NLT)

You Matter

We live in a fast-paced world where people long to feel important. You might strive to play a meaningful role in your family, your friend group, or at work. In today's society, importance is often measured by popularity and productivity. That may be how the world defines value, but God sees it in a different light.

As a single person, it can be especially challenging to feel significant. You might find yourself striving for someone's affection, longing to matter to someone in a special way. But when that affection is not returned—when they don't see you the way you hoped—it can be crushing. Questions start to creep in: *Am I not important? Am I not enough?*

You do not have to listen to those questions. The reality is that you *are* important and you *are* enough. God never ties your importance to how people treat you or the opinions they hold about you. Your value isn't determined by how hard you work or how much you strive to earn approval. You matter deeply, simply because you are His, and nothing can take that away.

Leah's story in Genesis 29 reveals this.

Leah knew exactly what it felt like to be second-best. In a deceptive scheme, she was given to Jacob in marriage, but he never truly loved her. His heart belonged to her younger sister, Rachel.

Can you imagine the devastation she must have felt? She was married, yet emotionally alone. Again and again, she gave birth to Jacob's children—each time hoping, *Now my husband will finally love me.*

When her first son, Reuben, was born, she said, *"Surely my husband will love me now"* (Genesis 29:32).

With her second, Simeon: *"Because the Lord heard that I am not loved, he gave me this one too"* (Genesis 29:33).

With her third child, Levi: *"Now at last my husband will become attached to me, because I have borne him three times"* (Genesis 29:34).

Leah was striving. She was doing everything she could to earn love, to prove her worth, to feel important to someone she cared deeply about. But time and time again, Jacob chose Rachel.

Something changed when she gave birth to her fourth son. Instead of reaching for Jacob's affection, she turned her eyes toward God and said: *"This time, I will praise the LORD"* (Genesis 29:35). She gave him the name Judah which means "to praise".

This one small sentence marked a breakthrough moment. Instead of seeking her husband's approval, Leah sought the Lord's. She began to realize that her value was not found in being loved by Jacob, but was grounded in being seen by God.

And here is what makes it extra special: Jesus—the Savior of the world—came through the line of Judah. God chose Leah—the overlooked sister, the unloved wife—to be part of His greatest redemption story. Gives you goose-bumps, right? God works in the most awesome ways!

Noticed and Valued

Longing to be chosen by someone who doesn't choose you back is not limited to romance. It can happen with a friend, a family member, or a co-worker. The ache of insignificance can appear in many different relationships.

Maybe you have been there. You are the friend who always shows up but never receives the first invitation. The employee who consistently goes above and beyond yet is overlooked for the promotion. The person who invests in someone hoping and praying they will recognize your worth.

You put your heart out there, only to feel invisible.

Be assured that you do not have to feel that way anymore. You have a God who notices and values you. He always sees you and He always chooses you. You are important to Him.

God has a long history of choosing the overlooked, the underestimated, and the brokenhearted to carry out His most beautiful work. He chose David, the youngest son and a lowly shepherd, to become king. He chose Gideon, who was hiding in fear, to become a mighty warrior. He chose Mary, a young, poor, small-town girl, to be the mother of the Messiah. And He chose the woman at the well, judged by so many, to become the first evangelist in her town.

Why did He choose them? He looked at their hearts. He saw their willingness, faithfulness, and humbleness. God doesn't measure worth by popularity, status, or titles. He looks inside your soul and knows every part of it, even parts that you may not know. He loves and accepts you just as you are.

That Little Voice

Before we can fully live in the truth of our worth, we must pause and take an honest look at what stands in the way. Sometimes it is the wounds from our past, the voices of insecurity, or the quiet doubts that cloud what God says is true. Other times, it is the constant pull of work, kids, and endless responsibilities that distract us from His voice. At the heart of it all, one of the most significant barriers is that little voice inside our own head—the one that says we are not enough.

I remember a moment when I caught myself thinking something I hadn't even consciously invited in. I was on my way home from work and needed to grab a few things from the store. Like most teachers, I was exhausted and ready to be home. The last thing I wanted to do was make a grocery run.

I pulled into the lot, parked, and got out of my car to start walking toward the entrance. Suddenly, right in the middle of the driving lane, I stopped walking. I had forgotten my purse. Without hesitation, the very first thought that hit me was, "You are so stupid, Angie! How could you do that?"

It was like time froze for a moment—not because I forgot my wallet, but because that voice in my head felt so sharp and automatic. That one thought carried tons of shame.

It just so happened that I was in therapy at the time, and this was something my therapist and I had been talking about: the power of that inner critic and how negative thoughts often run unchecked. I had heard the concept before, but I never truly noticed it happening in real time until that day.

From that moment on, I started to pay attention to what that little voice was saying. And let me tell you, it said a lot.

Thank God for therapy. I learned how to identify those automatic negative thoughts and how to reframe them with truth and grace. It takes practice, but once you start noticing the quiet lies, they begin to lose their power.

These thoughts sneak in so subtly that we often do not question them. We just accept them as truth. But they can be loud obstacles standing in the way of how God sees us. When you are single, hurting, or just longing to be seen, those lies can feel louder: *You're too broken. You're awkward. You're not important.*

If we are not careful, we start to believe the fibs. We internalize them. Over time, they shape how we see ourselves—so far away from how God sees us.

Another obstacle we often face is comparison. It is easy to fall into, especially with social media at our fingertips. Scroll for just a few seconds and you will see what looks like "perfect" couples, "perfect" families, and "perfect" holidays. It is easy to want what they seem to have.

But here is what we forget: We are usually only seeing the highlight reel. What we do not see are the silent battles they may be fighting behind the scenes. Most people post the good stuff: the smiling pictures, the celebrations, the fun. Rarely do they post the lonely nights, the arguments, or the moments when everything feels like it is falling apart.

Social media can be especially perplexing around the holidays. My two sons are grown and serve in the military. Due to deployments or work, they are not always at home. While others are posting pictures of big family gatherings, bright smiles, and full dinner tables, I sometimes sit in a quiet house—no pictures, no kids, no husband, no holiday chaos. Just me. In those moments, the enemy attempts to overwhelm me with a wave of sadness and isolation.

Comparison can be a sneaky thief. It creeps in slowly and steals our joy. We often don't even realize what is happening. Before we know it, whispers of inadequacy take hold. We are left viewing ourselves in a negative light.

How do we fight these invisible battles that we often don't realize exist? Here are a few practical ways:

Reframe the thought. Make a mental note when you catch a negative or comparison-filled thought. Write it down when you get the chance. Then, reframe it. Instead of saying, "I am all alone" say, "God is with me, and I am never alone." Speak the truth to yourself over and over until it becomes part of your thinking. What you repeat will begin to take root.

Limit social media time*.* Social media can feel like Satan's playground. It offers endless opportunities to compare ourselves to others. We are left feeling inferior or believe that we are missing out. If it starts to trigger discouragement or envy, it is okay to take a step back. Guard your heart, because what you feed it will grow.

Fill your mind with Scripture. God's Word is our strongest weapon and our manual for navigating life. Scripture is alive and grounds us in truth when lies try to creep in. It can be comforting to write out your favorite verses and post them where you will see them: the bathroom mirror, the fridge, your desk. Putting them in your daily vision will help you read and reflect multiple times a day. The more you see them, the more you will remember who you are and who you belong to. Scripture becomes a sword in the middle of the battle (Ephesians 6:17).

Masterpiece

Isn't it amazing that no two fingerprints are exactly alike? Out of the billions of people who have ever lived, not one has the same pattern as you. Your fingerprint is unique and the Creator of the universe crafted it with love and care.

You were not mass-produced. You are an original and handmade by God Himself. There's no copy of you. No substitute. No version 2.0. Just the one and only *you*.

Additionally, it's not just your fingerprint that is unique. God designed every part of you with intention: your voice, your laugh, your quirks, and your gifts. You are wonderfully made because you are irreplaceable in His sight. Your fingerprint leaves a mark. So does your life.

When we are single—especially for a long time—it is easy to feel flawed or invisible. We may look in the mirror and see someone who doesn't measure up. As we age, that feeling can grow. We might tell ourselves we are no longer attractive, interesting, or valuable.

But our Heavenly Father tells us otherwise. In Psalm 139:13-14, David praises God for the way He made us:

> *For you created my inmost being; you knit me together in my mother's womb. I praise you because I am fearfully and wonderfully made; your works are wonderful, I know that full well.*

God intricately designed each person. His craftsmanship was deliberate, detailed, and personal. Nothing about you is accidental. He does not make mistakes.

You are His masterpiece. From head to toe, you were created with care. And not just your physical traits—He also handpicked your talents, your personality, your dreams.

Every part of your being is seen, known, and lovingly used by God. You are made in His image (Genesis 1:27), woven together with divine intention. And even when you don't feel remarkable, your Maker says that you are.

My Prayer for You

Dear Jesus,

Thank You so much for creating this precious reader. I praise You for fearfully and wonderfully making them with purpose and care. When they feel low or question their importance, remind them that they are Your creation—a masterpiece that is uniquely created and deeply loved.

Amen.

Daily Affirmations

1. I am important.

2. My Heavenly Father wonderfully created me.

3. I know my worth.

Reflections

1. How does it change the way you see yourself, knowing that God is happy you exist?

2. Where in your life do you feel "less than," and how might God see those very places as beautiful and purposeful?

Chapter Six
You Have Purpose

*And we know that in all things God works for the good of those
who love him, who have been called according to his purpose.*
Romans 8:28

For Purpose, On Purpose

I enjoy all kinds of music: Christian, 80s, 70s, orchestra, musicals—you name it, I love it.

Music speaks to me in a way that words alone cannot. Some songs are meaningful and stir something profound. They bring joy, beauty, and tears. If a song gives me goosebumps on the drive home, I know it is special. It tugged on a heartstring somewhere.

I've been known to get those goosebumps when listening to an orchestra. Have you ever noticed just how many different instruments must come together to make such wonderful songs? During a symphonic piece, each instrument plays an individual part. On its own, that line might not sound like much. But when all the instruments combine, they create something breathtaking. Every part matters. One instrument may carry the melody while another plays a simple harmony or rhythm. Each one has a purpose, and it's only when they play together that the full beauty of the piece shines for all to hear.

I have been playing the violin for about five years and still consider myself a beginner. One day, my childhood best friend asked me to play background music while she sang a prelude at church. She has a stunning voice and a heart entirely devoted to worship. When she asked, my first instinct was panic: *There's no way I can do that.*

Up until then, the only person I had played with was my teacher, who accompanied me on the cello. Even then, my parts were simple—not quite "Mary Had a Little Lamb," but not much more advanced either.

Still, I told her I would try. She reassured me that no one at her church would mind if I hit a few wrong notes. We found the chords to the song, and she invited a friend to play guitar. So there we were—a little trio. My part? Simple, long notes in the background. Nothing fancy. Nothing impressive. If you had heard just my part alone, you might have thought a small animal was in distress. But when her voice, the rhythm of the guitar, and my simple notes came together, a joyful noise was made for the Lord. It sounded like one piece. It was beautiful.

Did I hit a wrong note or two? You better believe I did. My bow was shaking too. But the beauty wasn't in perfection. It was in participation. Those long notes I played sounded meaningless on their own, but they added depth and harmony to the music. They served a vital purpose.

And so do you.

You may not feel like the melody in God's song. You may think your role is too small or too quiet to matter. But that is not true.

In the symphony of God's story, every note counts. Without your important part, the song is incomplete.

He created you for a purpose. Your life has eternal meaning because you were designed with intention and love. God carefully crafted you with a role in mind. He didn't overlook you or forget to assign you a calling. He created you to fulfill a specific purpose on this earth—something only you can do.

And if your purpose feels small or behind-the-scenes in your single season, please hear this: It is not insignificant to our Heavenly Father. In His Kingdom, every role matters, including yours. Every act of obedience and participation counts.

Whenever I need to remember how intentional God is or how important I am to His plan, I think of one of my favorite verses—words that slow my anxious heart and remind me how carefully God holds my life:

> ***You saw me before I was born. Every day of my life was recorded in your book. Every moment was laid out before a single day had passed.***
> **(Psalm 139:16, NLT)**

God already knows the plans He has for you. You do not have to strive or stress to invent your purpose. He has everything mapped out. All you need to do is surrender, seek Him, and follow His leading.

Starting Point

Where does this purpose begin? And how do you discover what God designed you to do? Start with what He already placed inside you.

God has blessed you with desires in your heart. He knows your hopes, your gifts, and your passions. He sees the dreams you dare speak to anyone else. That's where purpose often begins—in the things you love and the places where your heart comes alive.

King David understood this and expressed it in Psalm 139:1–4 (NLT):

> *O LORD, you have examined my heart, and know everything about me. You know when I sit down or stand up. You know my thoughts even when I'm far away. You see me when I travel and when I rest at home. You know everything I do. You know what I am going to say even before I say it, LORD.*

Even when you feel unseen or unsure, God sees you clearly. He knows exactly how He wants to use you in every season of your life, including your single ones.

Let's look at Sarah, the wife of Abraham. Her heart desired to have a child. She waited so long that she had given up hope. She and Abraham laughed when God told them they would become parents in their old age (Genesis 18:10–12). True to His word,

Sarah gave birth to Isaac and became the mother of a great nation. Her waiting had good reasons. It was part of a bigger purpose.

Sarah wasn't the only woman who cried out for a child and found purpose in the process. Hannah, too, longed to be a mother. Her deep anguish poured out in prayer at the temple. She promised God that if He gave her a son, she would dedicate him to His service. God heard her prayer and blessed her with Samuel. He became one of Israel's greatest prophets (1 Samuel 1–2).

Their stories remind us: Purpose often begins with desire and is shaped through surrender, obedience, and trust. Sarah and Hannah did not rely on themselves. They relied on God.

Maybe you're reading this and thinking, *That's beautiful, but I'm still alone and single.*

Maybe you've asked questions like: *What if I never get married? What if I don't have children? What if I'm walking through life solo—does my purpose still matter?*

Yes. A thousand times, yes.

Your purpose is not on pause until you are married. It is not tied to your relationship status, family size, or stage of life. You are not a "less-than" version of God's creation because you are single.

The Bible is filled with individuals who walked closely with God and made an eternal impact without a spouse or traditional family. Jesus Himself lived a single life. Paul, who wrote much of the New Testament, was also single. He wrote that singleness could be a blessing, giving more time to please the Lord by doing His work (1 Corinthians 7:32-35).

There is no need to sit around waiting to be chosen by another person to begin walking in God's purpose. Your current season is a vital part of your purpose. Make yourself available to Him now and put your focus on Him. He will equip you with what you need and be with you every step of the way.

Now What?

Purpose doesn't usually hit with a lightning bolt or show up right away. It can unfold slowly, piece by piece, and grows as your relationship with God deepens. Spending time in scripture, prayer, and reflection will help foster the process. Here are a few ways to walk in your purpose:

Start where you are. Perfect circumstances are not required to start walking in your purpose. Do you know someone who might need a kind word? Are there opportunities to serve in your community? Did a Bible verse stir your heart? These are great places to begin.

> ***For God is working in you, giving you the desire and the power to do what pleases him.*** **(Philippians 2:13, NLT)**

Do the next right thing. Sometimes purpose looks like the next faithful step. Is God nudging you to invite your elderly neighbor over for coffee? Is there someone you need to forgive, encourage, or pray for? Whatever your "next right thing" is, trust Him and take that step.

The LORD makes firm the steps of the one who delights in him; though he may stumble, he will not fall, for the LORD upholds him with his hand. **(Psalm 37:23-24)**

<u>Use what you've got.</u> God often uses the very desires, skills, and personality traits He placed inside you. Are you creative? A good listener? Passionate about kids or music? Don't minimize your gifts. They may be an answer to someone's prayer.

God has given each of you a gift from his great variety of spiritual gifts. Use them well to serve one another. **(1 Peter 4:10, NLT)**

Take heart, my friend—God designed you with a specific purpose in mind. You are His masterpiece. You were made *with purpose* and you were made *on purpose*. Crafted with love, intention, and great care, your life carries meaning.

You can shine in this single season and in every season to come. Keep your eyes and heart fixed on Jesus. He will guide your steps, and your life will sing His melody of love.

My Prayer for You

Dear Father,

I ask that You bless this reader with a sense of how important they are to You. Help them to notice the stirrings you have placed in their heart. Guide them as they seek to understand their unique calling, and give them courage to walk confidently in the purpose You have set before them.

Amen.

Daily Affirmations

1. I was made for purpose on purpose.

2. I make a difference in God's Kingdom.

3. Even in seasons of waiting, God is shaping me for His purpose.

Reflections

1. What unique gifts or passions has God given to you that point to His purpose for your life?

2. When have your plans fallen through, but God worked something better out of it?

Chapter Seven

You Have a Part to Play

Now you are the body of Christ,
and each one of you is a part of it.
1 Corinthians 12:27

No Need to Wait

You have a starring role in the Kingdom of God—a role crafted uniquely for you. It reflects your heart, passions, purpose, and the person God designed you to be. This role is not dependent on your relationship status or title. Whether you are single, married, or widowed, God wants to use you *now*, not just in some distant "next."

As singles, we sometimes feel as if life hasn't truly begun. It is easy to slip into a mindset of "waiting." It could be waiting for a relationship, a spouse, or for something to make us feel like we have arrived. We may look around and wonder, *Do I have anything to offer the world as I am?* That feeling can be heavy. It can feel like a quiet kind of loneliness, a lingering sense that we are sitting on the sidelines of life, watching others live theirs. We might tell ourselves, *Once I have a partner, I'll step into that calling.*

But God's plans for you are not on pause. You do not have to wait to walk with purpose. You can step boldly into the role He has already written for you.

Your single season is part of a divine path. You can live fully, serve sincerely, and thrive joyfully right here, right now. Who knows? You might find that this season holds a kind of freedom and focus that makes it especially fruitful.

The Bible tells accounts of women and men who faithfully served God without being married. Their lives remind us that singleness is not to be a sidelined season. Instead, it should be a time of purpose and intimate partnership with God.

Jesus, our Savior, was single and lived the most meaningful life in history. He was a teacher, healer, and servant. He fulfilled His divine purpose completely without ever being married. His life modeled compassion, service, and an unshakable connection with the Father.

Paul embraced and celebrated singleness (1 Corinthians 7:7-8, 32–35). He called it a gift that allowed him the freedom to focus on the Lord, travel, preach, and write. As an apostle and church planter, Paul penned thirteen New Testament letters that continue to shape our faith today.

Mary Magdalene was a devoted follower of Jesus whose purpose was never defined by a relationship. She stood by Him in life and death. In a stunning moment of trust, God chose her to be the first witness of the resurrection—the most fantastic news ever.

Jeremiah, the "weeping prophet," was called by God to remain single because of the hardship of his mission (Jeremiah 16:2). He was tasked with delivering an unpopular message to a rebellious generation. Even in his isolation, Jeremiah remained obedient and emulated courage in the face of rejection.

Each of these lives teaches us something: Our relationship status does not determine our purpose. These men and women did not sit backstage waiting for the curtain to rise. With God's strength, they stepped boldly into the spotlight of their calling. They lived with courage, devotion, and intention—right where they were.

A Unique Freedom to Serve

We have 24 hours in a day. How we spend those hours changes with our season of life. In this current single season, I often find myself with a lot of empty time. My boys are now grown, living their own lives. The days of driving them to school, practices, and events are long gone. And truth be told, I miss those hectic days.

Now, I cook for one. I do laundry for one. I make most decisions—for one. It's just me navigating daily life. And suddenly, it feels like time has been handed back to me in big chunks. If I had a soundtrack playing, it would probably be that old song about having too much time on your hands. It feels fitting for this phase of life.

What if we changed our perspective and viewed this extra time not as a burden, but as an invitation to something wonderful? This season isn't just empty space. Though different, it holds special opportunities.

When we shift our focus, this extra time becomes full of unique freedom. Freedom to deepen our relationship with God. Freedom to serve. Freedom to say "yes" when He calls.

Without the daily responsibilities of marriage, many singles find themselves with incredible flexibility. There is more time for things like missionary travel, group Bible studies, community investment, and spiritual growth. The opportunities are abundant.

Anna the prophetess understood the opportunity of singleness. Though she lived alone for many decades, her life was far from empty or wasted. Luke 2:36–38 tells her remarkable story. She had been married for only seven years when her husband died. After that, she lived as a widow until the age of 84.

Anna did not let grief or loneliness define her story. Instead of withdrawing or merely existing, she dedicated her life to serving God at the temple. She never left the temple courts but worshiped there day and night through fasting and prayer. Her singleness was not a holding pattern. It was a holy offering.

When Mary and Joseph brought the infant Jesus to be presented, Anna was there. Led by the Spirit, she instantly recognized Him as the long-awaited Messiah. She responded with joyful praise and gratitude, and then began telling others about Jesus. She was one of the very first people to proclaim the good news.

Anna's life proves that we do not need a crowd, a stage, or a spouse to live a purposeful life. She did not waste her singleness by wishing it away or by waiting for her story to start again. She offered it to God and, in doing so, witnessed the arrival of the Savior with her own eyes. Her faithful, set-apart life speaks volumes: A quiet life can echo loudly in eternity.

Your singleness is not a mistake, a pause, or a placeholder. It is a space where beautiful things can grow. You can live a life filled with purpose and a spiritual connection to God. You do not have to wait for a spouse or a spotlight. You are already in a place where God can meet and use you to impact others.

What if you leaned into this season not with sorrow, but with divine intention? What if your prayers, faithfulness, and daily devotion are planting seeds that God will one day use to bring hope and redemption to others?

The world may overlook quiet lives, but God never does. Your life matters. Your worship matters. And your story can point others to Jesus.

Like Anna, you can use this season to serve fully. Her example shows that a life devoted to God can have an eternal impact, no matter how quiet or solitary. You too can use your single season to worship and serve. Here are some practical and powerful ways to begin:

Say Yes! Flexibility is a unique freedom of being single. Without having to coordinate with a partner, you have opportunities to respond to nudges from God. You can say "yes" to many things, such as helping a friend, jumping into a ministry at church, or delivering a meal to someone in need. Your availability is a gift. You can use it boldly and further the Kingdom of our Lord.

Spend time with God. Since you have fewer distractions, it may be easier to focus on God's presence. Use this time to develop a devotional rhythm, engage in uninterrupted prayer, or study

Scripture with intention. You could start a small Bible study with a few friends. These spiritual investments will ground you and bear fruit in future seasons.

Be flexible. You have more opportunities to be flexible with your time during this season, so use it intentionally. Shape your days around where God is leading you to grow, serve, or rest. Schedule time for renewal and refreshment. Let the Holy Spirit help you structure your time with eternal purpose in mind.

Pursue those passions and projects. That dream stirring in your heart? Now might be the time to chase it. Whether it's writing a book, starting a ministry, or volunteering for a cause, this season provides a unique opportunity to pour your time and energy into what God is calling you to build.

Build community. Singleness often gives you greater relational space. Use that space to foster friendships, invest in your family, or mentor someone young in the faith. God can use your availability to bring healing and wisdom to the lives of those around you.

Prioritize growth and healing. You can use this season to work on becoming whole. You have more time to heal past wounds and grow spiritually in Christ. Enlist the help of a counselor or trusted mentor. It isn't just preparation; it is transformation.

Be mobile for Kingdom work. This season can offer the kind of freedom others do not have. Whether it's a mission trip or an assignment outside your comfort zone, God may ask you to go. You might be more capable and prepared than you think to follow Him wherever He leads.

You do not have to wait for a future season to make an impact—this is your moment! What could happen if you fully embraced this time as sacred ground? Is it time to take that next step?

Don't Hesitate

Sometimes we hold back on stepping out because we are waiting for "later" or "the future."

Later, when we have a partner or spouse.

Later, when life feels more settled.

Later, when everything feels complete.

But friend, God is not waiting for later. He is inviting you *now*.

Don't let fear keep you stuck. You do not need a perfect life or flawless circumstances to walk in your purpose. Your value is not diminished by being alone. In fact, it is quite the opposite! You can live fully, right here, right now. This season of life is not a waiting room or a pause in your story. It's a launching pad for everything God has ahead.

God can do remarkable things through a heart that says "yes." He can use what He has already put there: your hopes, your gifts, your passions. Ask Him: *Father, how can I serve You right now? Show me what is already in front of me.*

So, what is one bold step you can take this week? Sign up to serve at your church or in your community? Start that Bible study that keeps tugging at your heart? Reach out to someone who needs encouragement or prayer?

Take the step. Offer what you have. Let God take care of the rest. You were not meant to sit this single season out. God delights in you—and He is calling you to live your days *fully*.

My Prayer For You

Dear Jesus,

Thank You for this season that my friend is in, even if it feels slow and quiet. Let them know that it isn't empty, but full of Your presence. Remind them that singleness isn't a time to sit on the sidelines: It's a time to use their gifts to bring hope to others. Give them courage to step forward to do Your will.

Amen.

Daily Affirmations

1. I am a valuable part of the body of Christ.

2. God has uniquely gifted me to serve in His Kingdom.

3. My role in God's Kingdom matters.

Reflections

1. How can I serve faithfully, even in unseen or "small" ways?

2. Who in my life can I encourage as part of my calling?

Chapter Eight

You Make a Difference

Therefore, my dear brothers and sisters, stand firm. Let nothing move you. Always give yourselves fully to the work of the Lord, because you know that your labor in the Lord is not in vain.
1 Corinthians 15:58

It's The Little Things

Have you ever paid it forward, like buying a stranger's coffee or covering someone's meal? The beauty in these seemingly small gestures is that they rarely stop with us. They often ripple outward and bless people in ways we may never know.

Take for example one Mother's Day when my young boys and I went out for lunch. At the end of our meal, I was surprised to find out that a couple next to us had quietly asked the server for our check. They insisted on paying for us. Since the couple purchased our meal, I was able to use the set aside lunch money as a generous tip for our shared waitress. This couple's kindness sparked more kindness.

There are other small instances in the world that illustrate this further. Think about a tiny acorn: It is barely noticeable at first, but over time, it grows into a towering oak tree that offers shade and shelter. Or picture a still pond: One single pebble tossed into the water creates rings that stretch far beyond the splash. And imagine a candle: A quiet flame is enough to brighten a room.

Examples like these remind us that faithfulness in the smallest of moments matter. They may not feel grand or impressive, but over time, they can change the world around us.

The good news? You don't need to be married or hold a special title to make an eternal impact. Whether you are single or in a relationship, your tiny yeses to God can ripple into someone else's miracle.

In John 6:1-15, we witness an event where something small becomes a miracle. It started on a mountainside near Bethsaida.

As Jesus and the disciples traveled, crowds of people began to follow. Word had spread of Jesus healing the sick. People came from all around to get a glimpse. Instead of pushing the crowds away, Jesus welcomed them with open arms. He taught them, healed their wounds, and showed compassion to all.

As the day wore on, the disciples became concerned. They urged Jesus to send the followers into the surrounding villages to find food and lodging. But Jesus had something else in mind. Turning to Philip, He asked:

> *"Where shall we buy bread for these people to eat?"* **(John 6:5)**

Philip, overwhelmed by the size of the crowd, replied that it would take more than half a year's wages just to give each person a bite. In other words: This is impossible.

Then another disciple, Andrew, spoke up. He had noticed a young boy with five small loaves of bread and two fish. He quickly dismissed the idea:

> *"How far will they go among so many?"* (John 6:9)

While the disciples doubted the boy's small offering, Jesus had a bigger plan. He took that small lunch and turned it into something extraordinary.

He instructed the crowd to sit down. Then, He took the loaves, gave thanks, and began to distribute them to the people. He did the same with the fish. Miraculously, *everyone* ate—not just a bite, but until they were full! Afterward, Jesus instructed the disciples to gather the leftovers. When the disciples finished, they had filled twelve baskets!

What started as a small, humble offering—a little boy's lunch—ended up feeding over 5,000 people that day. One act of giving and one ordinary lunch became a miracle in the hands of Jesus.

This account shows that God multiplies what we offer, no matter how small it may seem. We just need to be willing to bring it. When we surrender to Jesus, a small offering or a tiny act of kindness can have a ripple effect far beyond anything we could have imagined.

Maybe you feel like what you have to offer is not enough. Perhaps your resources seem limited—your time, influence, and finances.

Maybe in this season of singleness, you feel overlooked, like you're holding a lunchbox in a crowd of thousands.

Just remember this: God isn't asking you to feed the crowd. He is asking you to trust Him with what is in your hands. Like the boy with the loaves and fish, your offering may seem ordinary, but in the hands of Jesus, it becomes miraculous.

Whether it's your words of encouragement, your quiet prayers, or a small act of service—God sees it. He uses it. He multiplies it. Your "little" can feed many when you place it in His hands.

This Little Light

As a little girl, I loved to sing the simple song about a bit of light shining. I am sure you have heard the tune before. It's quite catchy!

Although children often sing it, the message is for everyone. It reminds us that we each carry a light within us. It is not a light we generate on our own. It is the light of Jesus—the Light of the World—shining through us. In Matthew 5:16, He said:

> ***"In the same way, let your light shine before others, that they may see your good deeds and glorify your Father in heaven."***

This verse states that our lights were created to shine for the purpose of reflecting the goodness of God. When people see our light, they see *Him*. This light isn't something we have to force. We *are* light because we *are* in Christ. His light is already inside us. Our job is to let it glow and not hide it away.

As believers, we are like lanterns in the night—pointing the way, spreading warmth, and revealing God's love. When we show kindness, patience, humility, and joy in our everyday lives, people take notice. They may wonder, *What makes her different? How does he stay so peaceful in tough times? Where does that hope come from?* In those moments, your light is reflecting the glory of the One who lives in you.

If you are struggling in your single season, do not allow sadness or loneliness to dim it. Instead, let it glow for all to see! Shining Jesus' light begins with small, everyday actions. Here are some easy ways to sit in the light of Christ, right in your daily walk:

1. Smile at strangers or say "hello." A warm smile can brighten someone's entire day. You never know what they are going through. Your actions might just change their outlook.

2. Speak words of encouragement. Use your words to lift others.

3. Be a good listener. Give your full attention to someone who needs to be heard.

4. Practice patience, especially in frustrating moments, such as traffic, long lines, or waiting for answers.

5. Offer help without being asked or expecting anything in return. Small acts of service can make gigantic impacts.

6. Give generously. Offer your time, talents, and resources to bless others.

7. Stay joyful in challenging moments. A peaceful heart can be a powerful testimony.

8. Compliment someone. Call out the good in others and let them know they are valued.

9. Invite someone to church or Bible study. Your invitation could be their first step toward hope and serve as an anchor point in their life.

10. Practice gratitude. A thankful spirit is contagious. Start a list of things you're grateful for.

Never underestimate how far a little light can reach, especially when God is the One shining through you. In your single season, you have a unique opportunity to respond to God's nudges by being more available with fewer distractions. He can do great things through your availability, openness, and faithfulness. He delights in using single hearts to bring His hope to those who need it most.

Hidden Fruit

We know it takes a long time for fruit to appear on a vine or tree. Grapes often take up to three years after planting to produce. Apple trees can take anywhere from three to six years to mature. Orange seedlings might not yield anything for seven to fifteen years.

Obviously, the process is a long one. Growth begins underground, in darkness and obscurity, long before anything breaks the surface. With the perfect combination of sunlight, water, and nutrients, deep root systems form and transformation unfolds quietly. We never know it is happening.

In the same way, the impact of our prayers, kindness, or service may not be immediately apparent or even in our lifetime. But that doesn't mean nothing is happening. The difference we make in others' lives may be hidden, slow, or completely invisible. But it is real. Even if you cannot see it, God is cultivating something good.

Let's look at a sweet account from the New Testament.

One day, Jesus was teaching in the temple and observing those who came to give their offerings. He watched as the wealthy people placed large amounts into the treasury chests. A poor widow approached and quietly dropped in two small copper coins, worth only a few cents. Jesus saw something far more profound than the amount she gave. He saw her heart.

> *Calling his disciples to him, Jesus said, "Truly I tell you, this poor widow has put more into the treasury than all the others. They all gave out of their wealth; but she, out of her poverty, put in everything—all she had to live on." (Mark 12:43–44)*

Her gift seemed small and insignificant, yet Jesus declared it immense in value. This widowed woman gave all she had, trusting God completely. She did not do it for attention or praise. She had no idea Jesus would notice.

But He did.

And He used her quiet act of sacrifice as a teaching moment for generations. What looked weak by worldly standards was great in God's eyes. Her story continues to bear fruit thousands of years later, reminding us of the beauty of hidden faithfulness and sacrificial giving.

Your labors may not produce fruit right away. In fact, you may never fully know the difference you have made. I often think about the many children I have taught who have now grown up. I wonder if I planted seeds that are still growing today. I consider the offerings I have given to my church, not knowing exactly how they were used or who they blessed.

Here is what I do know: God sees and He knows. He hears every prayer. He observes every quiet act of love. He weighs every offering—not by size, but by heart. When we give our time, our love, and our lives with genuine hearts, we are advancing the Kingdom of God even if we can't see it.

> **Let us not become weary in doing good, for at the proper time we will reap a harvest if we do not give up. (Galatians 6:9)**

It may be a harvest you don't see right away. Your fruit may not show immediately, but it is growing. And it is glowing with light in His Kingdom.

My Prayer for You

Dear Jesus,

Thank You for the one who is reading these words. Thank You for their desire to make a difference in Your Kingdom. Remind them that even when no one else sees their effort or quiet sacrifices—You do. You see their heart, and You treasure it deeply. In this single season, give them assurance they are impacting others who need Your love the most.

Amen.

Daily Affirmations

1. God has equipped me to make an impact.

2. My life shines His light.

3. My small actions make big differences.

Reflections

1. What gifts and strengths has God given you to advance His Kingdom?

2. How can you trust that God is working in the quiet moments of your life?

How You Live: Walking in Wholeness and Security

Part Three

You will keep in perfect peace those whose
minds are steadfast, because they trust in you.
Isaiah 26:3

Chapter Nine
You Are Complete

*Let perseverance finish its work so that you may
be mature and complete, not lacking anything.*
James 1:4

Complete in Him

A mosaic is a decorative art form that creates a larger image by arranging small, colorful pieces of material. These pieces are often shards of glass, tile, and broken pottery discarded from something once whole. They seem useless on their own, but in the hands of an artist, the fragments are carefully selected and positioned to form something breathtaking. The imperfections don't ruin the final product—they define it.

In many ways, our lives are mosaics. We carry scars, regrets, and moments that we wish we could erase or do over. As singles, we may be especially aware of what feels broken or missing. We might even believe that we need another person to be complete.

Praise God that we are already complete. When we belong to Jesus, we are not missing anything. He is the source of our identity and wholeness. He is the way, the truth, and the life (John 14:6).

There is no need to strive to fix the past or patch ourselves up to be more lovable or valuable. We are already made full with grace and love. What a wonderful reality!

Our lives are fulfilled in Him, yet society constantly says the opposite. We are pushed to chase more—more likes, more attention, more success. Thankfully, God is not like the world. He reminds us that we are whole in Him. He created us as masterpieces in His image—beautiful and complete.

Peace Within

Have you ever experienced those nights of constant worry and sleeplessness? I have. I've cried into my pillow and curled up in a corner of my room, feeling completely undone. In those moments, I felt restless and panicked. My thoughts spiraled as my heart seemed to beat out of my chest. There was little to no peace in my mind.

It took me a long time to discover why I felt so heartbroken. I realized that my pain was coming from trying to base my identity on someone else's opinion of me. And let me tell you: It never worked.

When I allowed another person to define my worth, I always came up empty—one hundred percent of the time. No human being can fill our hearts with peace and love the way that Jesus can.

So how can we cope with that kind of emotional pain and stress? How can we experience God's peace? It takes time, practice, and patience. A wonderful place to begin is the Holy Bible.

God speaks to us through His Word, bringing reassurance and understanding. It isn't just a book—it is a living blueprint for life.

All Scripture is God-breathed and is useful for teaching, rebuking, correcting and training in righteousness. (2 Timothy 3:16)

The Bible is our spiritual playbook. The more we read it, the more our thoughts, behaviors, and attitudes transform. It draws us closer to Jesus and quiets the chaos around us in a hectic and hurting world.

We will never find lasting peace in people, performance, or external achievements. Peace does not come from settling down with someone or finally having it "all together." True peace is internal. It comes from Jesus living within us. Our security is rooted in Him.

I still have hard days, and you will too. Sometimes, I feel the sting of loneliness at a group dinner where I'm the only single one. In those moments, I have learned that feelings are not facts. They are honest and painful, yes, but they are rooted in fear, not truth. And I get to choose how I respond to them. Here's what I do when those doubts creep in:

- I reflect on a verse the Holy Spirit brings to mind.

- I think of a song from my "Joy" Christian music playlist.

- I text a trusted friend and ask for prayer or encouragement.

- I listen for the still, small voice of the Holy Spirit, reminding me again: *You are loved.*

Our identity and peace are not something we have to earn or create. They are something we are. They flow from our connection with Jesus. He is with us, always.

> *"I am the vine; you are the branches. If you remain in me and I in you, you will bear much fruit; apart from me you can do nothing"* **(John 15:5).**

Just as a branch can't live or produce fruit without the vine, we can't thrive apart from Jesus. Staying connected to Him brings life, purpose, and internal peace—the kind the world does not offer and the kind that circumstances cannot take away.

Lies We Believe

At times, we wrestle with cultural messages and internal voices that echo: *You are incomplete. You will never be enough.* Society proclaims that we need abundant success, beauty, and relationships to be whole. The accuser knows precisely how to press into our insecurities. He targets the tender, vulnerable places in our hearts, hoping to reinforce the lies we have started to believe.

We do not have to accept those lies as truth. We are not powerless. We have Jesus. He told His followers:

"If you hold to my teaching, you are really my disciples. Then you will know the truth, and the truth will set you free" **(John 8:31–32).**

This promise is also for us. His truth has the power to undo lies, expose the enemy's schemes, and restore our sense of worth and identity. With Jesus, we don't just survive the lies—we overcome them.

Here are some internal lies that many singles hear and often start to believe. With Scripture as your foundation, you can replace every lie with a life-giving truth.

Lie: I'll be complete when I get married.

Truth: I am already complete.

Verse: *For in Christ lives all the fullness of God in a human body. So you also are complete through your union with Christ, who is the head over every ruler and authority.* (Colossians 2:9–10, NLT)

This verse assures that we are already made whole in Jesus. We don't need another person to "finish" us. We aren't waiting on anything else. We have Him.

Lie: If I were more successful, I'd be fulfilled.

Truth: True success is living in the love and purpose of Jesus Christ.

Verse: *You make known to me the path of life; you will fill me with joy in your presence, with eternal pleasures at your right hand.* (Psalm 16:11)

The presence of God is what fills us with true joy and lasting satisfaction. His presence is the path to peace.

Lie: Something is wrong with me because I am still single.

Truth: My relationship status does not define me; I am wonderfully made and fully known by God.

Verse: *For you created my inmost being; you knit me together in my mother's womb. I praise you because I am fearfully and wonderfully made; your works are wonderful, I know that full well.* (Psalm 139:13–14)

God designed you as a beautiful masterpiece. You are not lacking. Nor are you forgotten. There is nothing "wrong" with you. He sees you as His wonderful creation, just as you are.

Lie: When I finally have a partner, I'll be at peace.

Truth: My peace isn't dependent on a person. Jesus is my source of lasting peace right now, not someday.

Verse: *"Peace I leave with you; my peace I give you. I do not give to you as the world gives. Do not let your hearts be troubled and do not be afraid."* (John 14:27)

Jesus offers a peace that the world cannot replicate. Your relationship status does not delay His peace. You have access to it whether you are single, dating, or married. It is protective and present.

Ways to Stay Positive

You might be thinking, *Okay, I know the truth that I am complete and secure in Christ, but I still struggle.*

That is completely normal. Choosing joy and staying positive as a single person doesn't mean everything is easy. It means that you must strive to ground yourself in what is true when your emotions want to take over.

So how do we do that? How do we move forward on the hard days? How do we protect our hearts when sadness or discouragement creeps in?

There is a way. God has not left us to figure it out on our own. He has given us practical tools for staying secure in truth. These habits will anchor your joy, shift your focus, and help you walk in hope, even on the most challenging days.

Positive Affirmations: Start your day with truth. Use identity-focused Scriptures to speak life over yourself each morning. Write them on sticky notes and place them where you'll see them: your mirror, fridge, car, laptop, or phone. Let your eyes and heart be constantly reminded of who you are in Christ.

Truth Journal: Create a journal that focuses only on what God says about you. Write down His promises. Record your prayers. Pour out your heart and let your words be honest and raw. Then, speak them out loud. Hearing the truth in your own voice can help it settle deeply into your spirit. It becomes personal rather than distant.

Daily Prayer Time: Establish a regular time for prayer and Bible reflection. Ten minutes a day can make a big impact. Routine helps anchor your mind and spirit. Use apps, devotionals, or podcasts to guide you if you're not sure where to start. You don't have to do it perfectly—just begin, and God will meet you there.

Reach Out to a Friend: Don't walk through this alone. Reach out to a trusted friend, mentor, or family member who is grounded in faith. Let them in on how you're feeling. Vulnerability invites encouragement. Praying with someone brings the strength you need.

Listen to Worship Music: Fill your heart and space with uplifting worship songs that speak life into you. Let the lyrics remind you of who God is and how He sees you.

Practice Gratitude: Keep a gratitude list. Write down three things you're thankful for each day. Gratitude shifts your perspective and helps you focus on what God is doing in the present moment.

Create a Quiet Space: Designate an area in your home that is peaceful and free from distractions. Make it a space where you can sit quietly with God, reflect, and simply *be* in His presence.

Limit Comparison: Be mindful of the time you spend on social media. Unfollow accounts or pages that don't speak life into your soul. Choose instead to surround yourself with voices that point you toward God's truth and peace.

You don't have to wait for a future season to feel whole and secure. You are already deeply loved and complete in Christ. You are equipped to walk in peace *today*.

As you anchor yourself in Him, you will discover that joy fills your heart to the brim. Keep walking forward, knowing that God is with you and that your life is always full of meaning, beauty, and hope.

My Prayer for You

Dear God,

Please help this friend know that they are complete and secure in You. On days when they don't feel whole and insecurities rise, remind them of Your unchanging truth. Instill in their heart that they are defined by Your love rather than their relationship status. Help them rest in the peace knowing they are truly complete in You.

Amen.

Daily Affirmations

1. In Christ, I am complete. I lack nothing.

2. I am secure in my identity as God's child.

3. Nothing can separate me from the love of Christ.

Reflections

1. When you feel insecure, where are you placing your security instead of Jesus?

2. What areas of your life do you feel "incomplete," and how can you invite Christ into those spaces?

Chapter Ten
You Are Safe

"The Lord will fight for you; you need only to be still."
Exodus 14:14

Wrapped in His Love

Can you remember a time when you felt safe? Maybe you were huddled under a blanket during a storm, hidden away from the thunder. Or perhaps you were sitting in your grandmother's lap as a child, comforted by her heartbeat. Or it could have been a day when you came home after work, finally able to let down your guard and relax.

Small comforts give us a sense of being cherished and held. A feeling of peace amongst a hectic world. Blankets, arms, and homes bring temporary relief, but true and lasting protection comes from God.

The Bible is filled with reminders that God is not distant or detached. He is our refuge and defender. Our shelter in the storm. We are never exposed or abandoned. No matter what comes against us—fear, spiritual battles, unknown tomorrows—God's protection surrounds us like a shield. Scripture says that he will cover us with feathers and give us refuge under his wings (Psalm 91:4).

Life can sometimes leave us overwhelmed with a sense of not belonging. I recall nights when I felt especially sad and rejected. My natural response was to retreat—to curl up in a ball under the covers or, strangely enough, to sit in the small closet of my bedroom. I know that might sound odd, but there was something about being in a dark, tiny space that made me feel safe.

I sat motionless in the stillness, in the sadness, and in the tears. And yet, even there, I felt Him. I could not explain it, but I knew I wasn't alone. I was protected. His presence wrapped around me like a blanket.

God's protection doesn't always come in the form of escape or immediate resolution. Sometimes, it is a peace that finds us in the middle of mayhem.

I experienced that when my oldest son, who serves in the military, received a last-minute deployment after a significant world event. It was his first one like this. He only had two days to get everything ready, including packing up his entire apartment. His lease would end while he was away.

Those two days were some of the most chaotic I have ever experienced. Thankfully, I lived a short two hours away and was able to help. It was a whirlwind of stress, panic, and a heavy weight of uncertainty. But even as my emotions roller coastered, I sensed God's peace holding us together.

It came through scriptures that spoke truth to my heart; through worship songs that played during my drive to his town; through people God placed along the way. The military community became a living picture of God's protection.

One moment in particular stands out. The night before my son left, we went to a restaurant for dinner. We ran into a fellow serviceman who would be deploying with him. Leaving his own family meal, he came over to reassure me that he would look after my son. He'd been deployed several times and knew exactly what was ahead. In that moment, God's kindness showed up in a uniform.

In the apartment, we packed what we could, but there wasn't enough time to finish. After my son flew out, a handful of his coworkers and their spouses stepped in to finish the job. They packed the rest of his things and moved them into a storage unit they had reserved.

God was there. Amid the sadness, stress, and uncertainty, He surrounded us with love through peace in our souls and help from kind friends. His promises became more than words on a page; they were a fortress for our hearts.

Our Refuge and Fortress

Where can we turn when we feel unsafe, mentally drained, or less-than? What do we do when our hearts feel heavy? Who will protect us?

Our Heavenly Father.

His protection offers a peace that steadies us—a calm in the middle of a storm. Scripture says:

> *Whoever dwells in the shelter of the Most High will rest in the shadow of the Almighty. I will say of the LORD, "He is my refuge and my fortress, my God, in whom I trust"* (Psalm 91:1-2).

This verse gives two symbols of God's protection: a refuge and a fortress.

A refuge is a place of safety, shelter, and comfort. It is somewhere we can go when we feel scared, hurt, or in need of rest. It emphasizes gentleness and peace. Think of a quiet cabin during a storm or a hug after a hard day.

A fortress, on the other hand, brings strength to mind. It's a stronghold—a walled city or castle that can withstand attack. It represents defense, security, and power that surrounds and shields.

A refuge offers comfort. A fortress provides strength. And we need both.

God is our refuge, the One we run to for peace. He is also our fortress, the One who fights and defends us from what we cannot see. Both are essential. Together, they paint a complete picture of His protection: both tender and mighty, both gentle and unshakable.

His protection doesn't mean our troubles will disappear, but it does mean Jesus will be present in the middle of them. He will not leave us. Not ever. That is especially comforting when you are walking through a season without a significant other.

Singleness can carry its own kind of storms—those quiet ones that no one notices. The late-night thoughts and tears, the ache of feeling unwanted, the stress of handling everything on your own. It can feel like there is no one to lean on, no one to carry the load with you. But that is the exact spot where God steps in as both refuge and fortress.

> **The LORD is good, a refuge in times of trouble. He cares for those who trust in him. (Nahum 1:7)**

If you are single, this is not a lesser season. It is a wonderful time where you can experience God's protection in an incredibly personal way. You can be reassured that you are not navigating life alone—He is always with you. You are held, seen, and shielded by a God who never walks away.

Our Defender and Warrior

Along with being a refuge and fortress, God is our defender. He doesn't just shelter us: He actively fights for us, even when we can't see it. He is our warrior.

If you are carrying fears like abandonment, betrayal, or failure, put your hope and faith in God. He defends your heart and fights for you, just as He fought for His people throughout Scripture.

In Deuteronomy 31, we find the Israelites nearing the end of forty years in the wilderness. They were standing on the brink of hope, about to cross the Jordan River into the land God had promised them. Moses, their faithful leader, stood before them to explain what was coming. At 120 years old, he knew he would not cross, but assured the people that God would go ahead and prepare the way. In the face of uncertainty, Moses encouraged them:

> *"Be strong and courageous. Do not be afraid or terrified because of them, for the Lord your God goes with you; he will never leave you nor forsake you"* (Deuteronomy 31:6).

What a strong reassurance. What security it must have given the Israelites to know that they had a faithful Protector going ahead of them, fighting battles they could never fight on their own.

We also see this in the life of someone who we have discussed before: David. He was not a warrior by the world's standards. He was young, untrained, and overlooked. When he stood before the giant Goliath, he wasn't relying on armor or experience. He was confident that God would fight for him. He said:

> *"You come to me with sword, spear, and javelin, but I come to you in the name of the LORD of Heaven's Armies—the God of the armies of Israel, whom you have defied"* (1 Samuel 17:45, NLT).

David did not win because his strength. He won because God was with him.

The same God is with you.

You are not overlooked. And you are never defenseless. If singleness has left you feeling unprotected or unseen, remember that you are not on your own.

God sees every hidden fear and knows every quiet ache. He does not stand by silently. He steps in as your Defender and fights for your dignity. He guards your future. What others might overlook, God fiercely protects.

The promise He gave the Israelites is a promise for you too. Just as He went before them and just as He fought for David, He goes before you clearing paths, surrounding you and standing guard over your soul. He is a personal and active warrior that fights for you because you matter to Him.

Our Guardian

A shepherd has one primary responsibility: to protect his sheep. He doesn't just oversee them from a distance. He is involved in every detail as a caregiver, protector, and guide. He always keeps the flock's needs at the center of focus.

Some of his duties are simple like providing food and water. But others are more demanding, such as guiding them back when they wander or protecting them from predators.

Shepherding requires patience and fierce protection. It's not just a job. It is a calling of constant care and watchfulness. A good shepherd knows his sheep by name. He notices when one is limping, lags, or goes missing. And he does whatever it takes to bring them back.

God is our Good Shepherd. He watches over and cares for our souls just like a human one protects his sheep. He protects us, cares for us, leads us, and gives us strength. David wrote about this in Psalm 23: 1-4 (NLT):

> *The LORD is my shepherd; I have all that I need. He lets me rest in green meadows; he leads me beside peaceful streams. He renews my strength. He guides me along right paths, bringing honor to his name. Even when I walk through the darkest valley, I will not be afraid, for you are close beside me. Your rod and your staff protect and comfort me.*

These words are poetic and personal. David knew what it meant to tend, guide, and defend helpless sheep. So when he called the Lord his Shepherd, he was saying, *I trust You to care for me, just like I once cared for my flock.*

And centuries later, Jesus echoed this same imagery. In John 10:11 (NLT), He said:

> *"I am the good shepherd. The good shepherd sacrifices his life for the sheep."*

Jesus didn't just claim the title of Shepherd—He became the Shepherd. He is the One who laid down His life so that we could be safe and secure. He is not distant or passive. He is near and knows His sheep by name. He calls to us, protects us, and runs after us when we stray.

> **"If a man has a hundred sheep and one of them wanders away, what will he do? Won't he leave the ninety-nine others on the hills and go out to search for the one that is lost?" (Matthew 18:12, NLT)**

That one wandering sheep is important. It matters. *You matter.*

If shame ever leaves you feeling far off in any season of life, He will not scold or abandon you. He will search for you. He will find you. And He will happily lift you into His arms and carry you home. That is the heart of our Good Shepherd.

Maybe you feel like you have drifted. Maybe you have doubted that anyone notices. Know this: Your Shepherd sees and He's not content to let you stay lost. His desire is not to punish you. It is to protect you, to bring you home, and to remind you that you are still His.

My Prayer for You

Dear Heavenly Father,

Thank You for the soul whose eyes are reading these words. Remind them that they are safe and protected in Your arms. Assure them that You are near, and that Your protection surrounds them. Place a clear image in their heart of You as the Good Shepherd—the One who watches over them, cares for them, and brings them back when they stray.

Amen.

Daily Affirmations

1. God is my refuge and fortress.

2. God surrounds me with His protection.

3. I am sheltered under the shadow of His wings.

Reflections

1. Which promise of God's protection speaks to you right now?

2. What would it look like to rest in God's safety instead of trying to control your circumstances?

Chapter Eleven

You Are Forgiven

He has removed our sins as far from
us as the east is from the west.
Psalm 103:12 (NLT)

Playground Forgiveness

Have you ever watched two young kids playing together having a grand time when something suddenly goes wrong?

As an elementary teacher for 29+ years, I've seen this happen many times. On the playground, in the lunchroom, in the classroom—conflicts pop up constantly. Someone doesn't take turns. Another spills a drink. Someone knocks over a carefully built tower of blocks. For a six or seven-year-old, these moments feel enormous.

The reactions usually follow a similar pattern: tears, angry words, and sometimes storming off in frustration—big feelings over small things. But what always amazes me is what comes next.

More often than not, the child who caused the upset walks back over, gives a little hug and says, "I'm sorry." And without hesitation, the other replies, "I forgive you." Just like that, everything is back to normal again. They continue playing as if nothing ever happened.

These little moments are sweet to watch. Kids are quick to forgive. No lecture. No repayment required. Just forgiveness and grace.

And it makes me wonder: Isn't that what our hearts long for? To be able to start over? To be fully known and loved, mess and all?

What if forgiveness isn't about fixing yourself, but about letting someone else wash it all away?

That is what Jesus offers us—not just a clean slate, but a whole new life. Forgiven and washed clean.

Personal Invitation

You may know about Jesus, but maybe no one has explained why His life and death matter.

The Bible shows us how every person falls short of God's perfect standard. This dates back to the book of Genesis, specifically to the Garden of Eden. Adam and Eve chose to disobey God, and this decision severed the relationship they had with Him. From that moment onward, humanity has wrestled with separation from God.

Thankfully, we don't have to remain separated from Him. God gave us His beloved Son: Jesus. The gap is gracefully bridged through Him.

Jesus lived a perfect, sinless life. In a love beyond our understanding, He gave Himself on the cross, taking on every sin so we wouldn't have to bear it alone. Through His sacrifice, we are welcomed into a restored relationship with our Heavenly Father.

Three days after His crucifixion, Jesus rose from the grave, conquering sin and death, once and for all. Because of this, anyone who puts their trust in Him is forgiven.

Our salvation is both forgiveness and transformation. Past failures do not define us. Neither does our relationship status. We are made new in Jesus (2 Corinthians 5:17).

In other words, we are not just saved *from* something—we are saved *for* something.

For love.

For purpose.

For life with Him—now and forever.

If you have never accepted Jesus into your heart, I want to invite you to do it right now. He isn't distant or uninterested. He has been waiting for this moment with open arms. When you say yes to Him, angels sing.

You don't need perfect words. You just need a willing heart. If you would like to begin a relationship with Jesus today, you can pray something like this:

> *Dear Jesus,*
> *I know that I'm a sinner and I need Your forgiveness. I believe that You died on the cross for my transgressions and rose on the third day to give me eternal life in Heaven. Right now, I invite You into my heart. I trust You as my Savior and choose to follow You as my Lord. Thank You for loving me, forgiving me, and making me new. Help me to walk with You every day. In Jesus' name, Amen.*

If you prayed that prayer today, welcome to the family of God! Heaven is rejoicing! You are a beloved child of the King, completely forgiven, entirely accepted, and made whole in Him.

You are beginning a beautiful journey with Jesus! Start spending time in His Word with just a few verses a day. Talk to Him like you would to a friend. Find a Bible-teaching church or someone you trust to walk alongside you in faith. You are never alone.

God sees you.

He chose you.

And now, He lives in you.

Freedom Will Come

Enormous weights on our shoulders bring us down, both physically and mentally. It happens after finishing a big test or wrapping up an important presentation. That sigh of relief—the deep breath of finally being done—feels amazing, right? Walking in spiritual freedom is like that, but on a much deeper scale.

When you invite Jesus into your heart and repent of your sins, you are fully forgiven. The burden of shame and guilt no longer belongs to you because Jesus already carried it to the cross. You're not defined by your past anymore.

> *It is for freedom that Christ has set us free. Stand firm, then, and do not let yourselves be burdened again by a yoke of slavery.* **(Galatians 5:1)**

Picture a baseball uniform caked in red mud after a rainy game—stained and filthy. Now imagine it being washed thoroughly, treated with every powerful cleaner available, and coming out white as snow. That's what Jesus does with our sin. He takes it away and washes us clean. God says:

> *"Though your sins are like scarlet, they shall be as white as snow; though they are red as crimson, they shall be like wool"* **(Isaiah 1:18).**

Because of this, you do not have to continue punishing yourself. You are not meant to live in fear or regret. Jesus paid the full price for your freedom, and that means you are free to walk away from old patterns and destructive habits. In John 8:36, He says:

"So if the Son sets you free, you will be free indeed."

Walking in freedom is more than just a feeling; It is a fresh way of life. It is about walking daily with a Father who loves you and wants a relationship with you. You have a new identity in Christ

Living saved means it is time to let go of guilt, shame, and the need to punish ourselves. The enemy does his best to keep those lies stuck in our minds, but with your salvation, you are not stuck anymore. With God's grace, strength, and love, you can move forward in freedom.

So now there is no condemnation for those who belong to Christ Jesus. And because you belong to him, the power of the life giving Spirit has freed you from the power of sin that leads to death. **(Romans 8:1-2, NLT)**

If you are single, this part of freedom can be extremely personal. Maybe someone broke your heart. Perhaps you were misled, left behind, or overlooked. Maybe you're carrying anger, grief, or regret—questions like *Why didn't it work out?* or *Why not me?*

Forgiveness in singleness can mean releasing the person who hurt you. It can mean forgiving someone who didn't choose you, or even forgiving yourself for past decisions. Sometimes, the pain is great, but Jesus is greater.

It does not mean saying what the other person did was okay. It means you are handing that pain over to the One who already carried it for you. Jesus understands betrayal, rejection, and loneliness because He experienced them. And He knows how to redeem every ache and pain into something beautiful.

Some wounds leave scars, yes, but in Christ, scars do not define you. They remind you that you have been healed. They no longer intimidate or control you. Letting go of resentment and regret is part of living free. And in that freedom, you are not just surviving—you are becoming.

This freedom brings peace, joy, and living each day surrendered to Jesus. It leads to fulfilling the purposes that God has planned specifically for us. Now that we are seeking to glorify Him, we walk in His strength and strive to honor Him in all that we do. Our desires and His will begin to align.

Can you feel that weight lifting? It is the power of Christ's love and true freedom.

My Prayer for You

Dear Jesus,

Thank You for the gift of salvation—how wonderful You are to give Your life to save ours. Because of You, we are no longer chained to past guilt or shame. You have washed it all away. Help us to remember that singleness does not make us less saved or less loved. It is a time to grow deeper in relationship with You. Strengthen us to live in the joy of being free.

Amen.

Daily Affirmations

1. I am set free by His grace.

2. I am made anew in Christ.

3. I am forgiven.

Reflections

1. How has God's forgiveness set you free from guilt and shame?

2. Are you living in the daily reality of God's grace, resting in the fact that you are loved and forgiven?

Chapter Twelve

You Belong

*The LORD appeared to us in the past, saying: "I have loved you
with an everlasting love; I have drawn you with unfailing kindness."*
Jeremiah 31:3

The Deepest Longing

Imagine sitting alone at a wedding. People around you are laughing and clinking glasses. Spouses are holding hands. Couples dance beneath strings of lights. You are genuinely happy for the newlyweds, but something inside wonders: *Will I ever belong to someone like that? Will I ever matter to a spouse?*

Next, picture someone walking into an empty house after a long day of work. There's no one to ask, "How was your day?" No one to share the highs or the lows. No one to help decide what's for dinner. Just silence. And the ache of wishing someone—anyone—was there.

These aren't just hypothetical scenes. They are the lived experiences of many people. I have experienced them, and maybe you have too.

These aches reveal an unspoken feeling: We want to belong. Our innate desire is to be chosen, included, and known. When belonging feels uncertain or inconsistent, we learn to guard our hearts. We hold back and become cautious with our hope.

Consciously or unconsciously, we strive to be "good enough" to earn love or approval from others. We brace our hearts and minds for rejection. We fear that even if we are included for a while, we will eventually wear out our welcome. But our Heavenly Father leans in with compassion and without hesitation declares, *You belong.*

With my adult children living independently and a remote job that allows me to work from anywhere, I have been longing to move closer to my family and home. It isn't that I am unhappy where I am. I genuinely love my area with its sandy beaches, close friendships, and wonderful community. I have been here for 15 years and in many ways, it is home. My boys claim this to be their "hometown."

But even so, there has been a growing pull in my heart to be near family and to feel that familiar sense of belonging. I feel like it is time to change my view—literally. I am embracing a new season of life.

I have prayed about this move for several years now. When I look back through old journal entries and prayer lists, I see this decision pop up again and again. There are notes written in the margins with hopes and dreams.

Through all of those prayers, I have come to realize something important: This desire isn't just about zip codes or old memories. It is so much more. It is about feeling connected and being "home."

God offers connection to each of us. True belonging is found in His love. Belonging to Him is constant, stable, and steady. It isn't dependent on circumstances or your relationship status. It does not fade with time or change with other people's choices. Ultimately, no matter where we live or who we are with, we are His.

Whether surrounded by loved ones or standing in an unfamiliar place, God's love anchors us. His heart is our home. He has always been and will always be "our dwelling place throughout all generations" (Psalm 90:1).

Known Completely

As solo people, it is easy to find ourselves seeking acceptance in the wrong places or from the wrong people. We feel a need to belong to someone, some group, or some place. We don't want to do life alone. We want to "fit in" with our couple friends. We may desire to come home to a warm body at the end of a long day.

But putting our hope in the wrong person or chasing comfort in a relationship can leave us deeply disappointed and unfulfilled. It can also lead to dark spaces and bad situations we would never want to be in.

Thankfully, we do not have to wear a wedding ring or be a part of a group to be fully known and fully loved. God's love isn't reserved for the coupled or connected. It is for everyone. Your identity is founded in Him. His forgiveness has secured your place, and His love has claimed your heart.

And who exactly is He? He is the God who stays. He is the One who never leaves.

When others disappoint you, seasons shift, or relationships change, His love remains. Always. It is not occasional or performance-based. It isn't given in only your strong times or withheld in your struggling ones. God's love is steady, constant, and personal. It reaches into the most ordinary days and the most painful nights. It is purposeful and focused with your name written on it.

You have searched me, LORD, and you know me. You know when I sit and when I rise; you perceive my thoughts from afar. You discern my going out and my lying down; you are familiar with all my ways. **(Psalm 139:1-3)**

And I am convinced that nothing can ever separate us from God's love. Neither death nor life, neither angels nor demons, neither our fears for today nor our worries about tomorrow—not even the powers of hell can separate us from God's love. No power in the sky above or in the earth below—indeed, nothing in all creation will ever be able to separate us from the love of God that is revealed in Christ Jesus our Lord. **(Romans 8:38–39, NLT)**

God's promises are always good. Our Heavenly Father cherishes you. It is in His nature to pour life and affection into your heart.

He is with you when situations get quiet or complicated. He keeps track of you in the crowd. And when you feel overlooked or invisible to others, you are fully seen and deeply loved by Him.

If you have ever felt invisible as a single person, remind yourself that God has not passed you by. He is not waiting for you to get your act together, or for someone to put a ring on your finger before pouring out His affection. He knows every detail of your life, and He delights in walking with you through it all.

Love That Pursues

When you find yourself in that dark hole of sadness or when you start to believe the lie that you are unlovable, remember this: You are immensely loved by God, so much so that He gave His Son to save you. That is the greatest act of love.

If you still need proof of how personal and unwavering His love is, just look at the disciple, Peter.

Peter had been one of Jesus' closest friends. He was bold, passionate, and intensely loyal—or so he thought. On the night Jesus was arrested, fear overtook him. Not once, not twice, but three times, Peter denied even knowing Jesus.

And when the rooster crowed—just as Jesus said it would—Peter realized what he had done. Scripture says he went outside and wept bitterly (Luke 22:62). Can you imagine the depth of his regret? The shame? The sinking feeling that he had ruined everything?

Mercifully, Jesus did not leave Peter in that shame.

John 21:1-19 tells us that Jesus went in search of Peter and the disciples after the resurrection. On the shore of the sea, Jesus met him with compassion. He did not rebuke him. Instead, He asked, *"Peter, do you love Me?"*

He asked three times, mirroring Peter's three denials. Each time, Peter said, *"Yes, I love you, Lord."* And each time. Jesus responded with grace: *"Feed My sheep."*

It was a call to step back into love. Back into purpose. Back into belonging. Jesus was saying: *I still want you. I still love you. You still belong to Me.*

That is what God's love looks like. His goodness pursues us and brings restoration. Even when we give up on ourselves, God does not.

Living Loved

Being single can feel especially challenging. In a moment when you think you are doing okay, an unexpected wave of emotion might rush in. Sadness, loneliness, and the ache of longing can surface without warning. You may find yourself stuck in a fog, especially on quiet days when nothing seems to be moving forward.

You can be certain that hard days will come with storms in your life. That is a guarantee. But even in this silence and stillness, you are not alone. The God who created the universe is with you in every single moment. He sees you. He knows your heart. And He loves you—*completely*.

Living loved changes everything. When the ache unexpectedly comes to the surface, anchor yourself in the fact that you are abundantly and unconditionally loved. His love brings peace when anxiety creeps in and confidence when insecurity whispers lies. When you live loved, you stop striving for worth and begin resting in grace.

Even when you don't feel His nearness, I promise you—He is there. His love isn't based on your performance or emotions. It is steadfast.

So cling to Him.

Pray.

Be honest with God—He can handle your heartbreak.

Open your Bible and soak in scriptures about His love.

Talk with a trusted friend who can remind you of the truth.

Write out your feelings. Pour them onto paper and into His presence.

He invites you to remain in Him, because that is where your heart will find its home. He lavishes His children with perfect, unconditional love (1 John 3:1). He never lets go. And the more you lean into accepting that, the more your heart will heal and flourish.

Come Home

No matter where you are in life, you are wanted by God. You are fully loved and eternally welcome.

There is something comforting about coming home, not just to a place, but to the arms of the One who loves you most. No matter how far you have wandered, how much time has passed, or how messy your story feels, the invitation still stands: *Come home.*

Jesus once told a story to illustrate the scope of the God's love. It is the story of a son who left his father's house to chase freedom on his own terms. He took his inheritance early and squandered it all in reckless living. Eventually, he found himself broke, starving, and filled with shame.

He decided to go back home because he had nowhere else to turn. He rehearsed an apology in his head, hoping maybe he could be a servant in his father's house.

But that is not what happened. Jesus tells us:

> *"But while he was still a long way off, his father saw him and was filled with compassion for him; he ran to his son, threw his arms around him and kissed him"* (Luke 15:20).

The father did not offer a lecture or a list of demands. He didn't shame his son or ask him to prove himself. He ran. He embraced and completely restored him. No questions asked.

Maybe you have wandered in your thoughts, your choices, or your faith. Perhaps life took you down a path you never expected. Or maybe you are weary and unsure how to find your way back. No matter the reason, your Father is not angry. He is waiting with open arms.

Coming home means stepping into grace and sitting in love instead of striving for approval. It means knowing you do not have to fix everything first. You just have to come. He sees and delights in you. And He is already running toward you.

My Prayer for You

Dear Jesus,

Bless the one whose eyes are reading these words. Wrap them in the truth that they belong to Your family—fully known, fully forgiven, and deeply loved. May they sense Your open arms welcoming them home. Let them live each day anchored in grace. Let Your love be the safest place they know.

Amen.

Daily Affirmations

1. I belong to Jesus.

2. I am God's child.

3. I am never alone.

Reflections

1. How does your sense of identity shift when you remember you are a new creation in Christ?

2. What lies or labels about yourself do you need to let go of so you can rest in your belonging to Jesus?

Walk With Confidence
Closing

So then, just as you received Christ Jesus as Lord, continue to live your lives in him, rooted and built up in him, strengthened in the faith as you were taught, and overflowing with thankfulness.
Colossians 2:6-7

Walking With Jesus

You have turned each page and read every word. I hope you have highlighted some stuff too! I pray that you have felt recurring themes of security, peace, and hope on our journey together. Most importantly, I pray that you know how much Jesus loves you. His love is not conditional. It doesn't depend on your relationship status, your past choices, or how well you think you measure up. It is steady, unchanging, and personal.

When you first opened this book, did you feel the weight of questions? *Am I enough? Do I matter? Did God forget about me?* I hope that now, as you close this final chapter, you can hold onto a set of realities that will not waver: *You are chosen. You are whole. And you belong to Jesus.*

The world often sends singles a defeating message that life does not fully begin until you find a partner or spouse. But God's Word says something different. Your life is meaningful and happening right now in the present. You do not need to wait for another person to complete you because you are already complete in Christ (Colossians 2:10). You are not overlooked or forgotten; you are engraved on the palms of His hands (Isaiah 49:16). You are not wandering alone. Jesus Himself promises,

> ***"And surely I am with you always, to the very end of the age" (Matthew 28:20).***

One of the most significant turns in the Christian life occurs when you stop striving to *earn* your identity and begin living *from* the identity God has already given you. You belong to Jesus and can stand on the foundation of that love every day.

Paul reminds us in Romans 8:38-39 that nothing will separate us from His love. Not death. Not life. Not angels or demons. Not the present or the future. NOTHING. Period. End of story.

Think of it like this: The world hands you sticky notes with labels such as "single," "not enough," and "unwanted." But Jesus takes those off and replaces them with permanent marker: "beloved," "chosen," and "mine."

You do not have to base your worth in relationships or the approval of others. You can breathe and rest. You can know that right here, right now, you are fully known and fully loved.

Living With Confidence

Sometimes singleness feels like a waiting room, but it was never meant to be that way. You are already in the middle of God's story for your life. There is no need to put your calling on hold. The kingdom of God is here and now. You have a very important part to play. Paul's words in Ephesians 2:10 remind us:

For we are God's handiwork, created in Christ Jesus to do good works, which God prepared in advance for us to do.

That is true for every believer—single or married. Your purpose is not delayed. It is unfolding daily as you walk with Him.

And let's be honest: There will be hard days. You will have instances when loneliness presses in, when wedding invitations stir up ache, and when you wonder if God has forgotten your desires.

Thankfully, you don't have to deny those feelings to walk in faith. Jesus meets you there. The same Savior who wept at Lazarus's tomb (John 11:35) understands your tears. The same God who promised never to leave you (Deuteronomy 31:6) is present in your quiet and sad moments.

When the enemy shouts lies of insignificance, fight back with God's Word. Follow Jesus' example. He relied on God's word when facing temptation in the wilderness (Matthew 4). Scripture is powerful. It is a weapon of truth and will set your heart free.

On those difficult days, speak God's words over your heart. Write down affirmations and say them out loud if you need to:

- I belong to Jesus, and nothing can separate me from His love.

- My relationship status does not define me; Christ defines me.

- I am never alone; God is always with me.

- I have a purpose today, not just someday.

Even though we belong to Jesus first and foremost, He designed us to live in community. Instead of living in isolation, surround yourself with people who speak positively into your life and remind you of who you are in Christ. We need people who will pray with us, laugh with us, encourage us, and even challenge us when we forget our worth.

Being single does not mean being alone. It means we get to experience friendship, mentorship, and spiritual family in a way that often grows richer because of our availability to invest.

Your story may include marriage one day. Or perhaps it won't. Either way, your hope is not in a future spouse—it is in a faithful Savior. That hope is secure.

Jeremiah 29:11 is often quoted to remind us of peace and God's road map for our lives:

"For I know the plans I have for you," declares the LORD, "plans to prosper you and not to harm you, plans to give you hope and a future."

That future is not vague or uncertain—it is anchored in Christ. He holds your days and already knows your tomorrows. You do not have to walk in fear. Instead, you can walk confidently with your head held high and peace in your heart. Your worth is settled and your belonging is secure in Him.

Final Affirmations

Before we say goodbye and close the pages, I want to remind you of who you are in Jesus:

- God chooses you.

- You are complete.

- Jesus will never let you go.

- You are loved beyond measure.

- You have hope and a future.

My dear friend, this may be the end of these pages and our time together, but it is not the end of your story. This is an exciting beginning with the Heavenly Father as your Author.

Every morning is a new day, and every step is part of the journey. Walk forward with confidence knowing you are chosen, adored, forgiven, and free. You are a completed masterpiece who is deeply loved and adored by the Creator of the Universe. Nothing—absolutely nothing— will ever take that away.

Closing Prayer

Dear Heavenly Father,

Thank You for every person who has journeyed through these pages. Thank You for meeting them here and for reminding them who they are in You. Help them carry these truths beyond this book and into their everyday lives. When they feel alone, remind them that You are with them. When they doubt their worth, remind them that they are chosen, adored, and deeply loved. When they wonder about their purpose, guide their steps and light their path. Teach them to see singleness not as a deficit, but as a beautiful season filled with meaning, growth, and joy. Root their identity in Christ alone. Let Your love be the foundation they stand on, the security they rest in, and the joy that fuels their days.

Amen.

Daily Affirmations

<u>Chapter One: You Are Rooted in Love</u>

1. I am grounded in God's unwavering love.

2. God's love is not based on my relationship status.

3. I am fully known by my Heavenly Father.

<u>Chapter Two: You Are Chosen</u>

1. God chooses me.

2. I am not overlooked or forgotten.

3. I am handpicked by Jesus.

<u>Chapter Three: You Are Seen and Heard</u>

1. God sees me.

2. God hears me.

3. I am valued.

Chapter Four: You Are Adored

1. God adores me.

2. Jesus delights in me.

3. I am the apple of His eye.

Chapter Five: You Are Important

1. I am important.

2. My Heavenly Father wonderfully created me.

3. I know my worth.

Chapter Six: You Have Purpose

1. I was made for purpose on purpose.

2. I make a difference in God's Kingdom.

3. Even in seasons of waiting, God is shaping me for His purpose.

Chapter Seven: You Have a Part to Play

1. I am a valuable part of the body of Christ.

2. God has uniquely gifted me to serve in His Kingdom.

3. My role in God's Kingdom matters.

Chapter Eight: You Make a Difference

1. God has equipped me to make an impact.

2. My life shines His light.

3. My small actions make big differences.

Chapter Nine: You Are Complete

1. In Christ, I am complete. I lack nothing.

2. I am secure in my identity as God's child.

3. Nothing can separate me from the love of Christ.

Chapter Ten: You Are Safe

1. God is my refuge and fortress.

2. God surrounds me with His protection.

3. I am sheltered under the shadow of His wings.

Chapter Eleven: You Are Forgiven

1. I am set free by His grace.

2. I am made anew in Christ.

3. I am forgiven.

Chapter Twelve: You Belong

1. I belong to Jesus.

2. I am God's child.

3. I am never alone.

Reflections

<u>Chapter One: You Are Rooted in Love</u>

    1. Are there quiet places in your life where you can pause and experience God's presence?

    2. How does knowing you are rooted in God's love affect the way you view your worth?

<u>Chapter Two: You Are Chosen</u>

    1. What truth from this chapter speaks most to your heart?

    2. How can you walk confidently knowing that God chooses you?

<u>Chapter Three: You Are Seen and Heard</u>

    1. Which person in this chapter do you identify with most?

    2. How does knowing that God sees and hears you help you in your current season?

<u>Chapter Four: You Are Adored</u>

    1. How can knowing God adores you change the way you view your single season?

2. Picture Jesus' face lighting up when He sees you. Write down what you imagine He would say to you in that moment.

Chapter Five: You Are Important

1. How does it change the way you see yourself, knowing that God is happy you exist?

2. Where in life do you feel "less than?" How might God see those places as beautiful and purposeful?

Chapter Six: You Have Purpose

1. What unique gifts or passions has God given to you that point to His purpose for your life?

2. When have your plans fallen through, but God worked something better out of it?

Chapter Seven: You Have a Part to Play

1. How can I serve faithfully in unseen or small ways?

2. Who in my life can I encourage as part of my calling?

Chapter Eight: You Make a Difference

1. What gifts and strengths has God given you to advance His Kingdom?

2. How can you trust that God is working in the quiet moments of your life?

Chapter Nine: You Are Complete

1. When you feel insecure, where are you placing your security instead of Jesus?

2. What areas of your life do you feel "incomplete," and how can you invite Christ into those spaces?

Chapter Ten: You Are Safe

1. Which promise of God's protection speaks to you right now?

2. What would it look like to rest in God's safety instead of trying to control your circumstances?

Chapter Eleven: You Are Forgiven

1. How has God's forgiveness set you free from guilt and shame?

2. Are you living in the daily reality of God's grace, resting in the fact that you are loved and forgiven?

Chapter Twelve: You Belong

1. How does your sense of identity shift when you remember you are a new creation in Christ?

2. What lies or labels about yourself do you need to let go of so you can rest in your belonging to Jesus?

About the Author
Angie C. Austin

Angie C. Austin is a Christian, mom, and teacher passionate about helping people see their worth and identity in Christ. She writes for anyone who has ever felt overlooked, stuck in a season of waiting, or tempted to measure their value by others. Through Scripture, honest reflection, and personal stories, she encourages readers to embrace God's unchanging love and walk confidently in their purpose.

Angie is a graduate of Troy University and a lifelong resident of Alabama. She enjoys spending time with family and friends, traveling, reading, and noticing the ways God meets people in everyday moments. Her hope is that readers will leave her work with a renewed sense of God's love and the confidence that they are never forgotten or alone.

Connect with Angie: halenpress26@gmail.com

If you enjoyed reading this book, share a photo on social media using #SoloKnownLoved.